How to WIN at Racquetball

by Victor I. Spear, M.D.

 Rand McNally & Company

Chicago • New York • San Francisco

Second printing, February 1978

About the Author

Dr. Victor I. Spear is a graduate of the University of Michigan Medical School, Class of 1959. He is a practicing physician in Rockford, Ill., and a racquetball player.

His accomplishments in the latter field include reaching the semifinals of the Rockford City Championship for five consecutive years, and winning the championship in 1972 and 1974. He has never competed in regional competition outside of Rockford, with one exception: The 1976 Tri-City (Rockford-Beloit-Janesville) Tournament in Janesville, Wisc., in which he won first place.

He is **no** great athlete. But, then again, neither was Casey Stengel, Bobby Fischer, nor Arnold Palmer's father.

One more thing: He won first place in the first annual Ann Arbor City Chess Championship, 1961, as well as several other chess tournaments. That may be more pertinent to this book than you might think at first glance.

Table of Contents

Introduction

The first time I considered the possibility of writing an instructional book on racquetball strategy, the idea was quickly, almost shamefully, dismissed. After all, I thought, only professionals write such material, because they have the skills and the trophies to back it up. It seemed so presumptuous for a no-name, non-athlete, nobody player from a town of 160,000 to be advising other players on how to play the game. But as I began to pursue the idea further, something else occured to me. The most competent surgical instructors are not necessarily the greatest surgeons, themselves. The more I thought about it, the more obvious it became. Teaching and performing are totally different skills.

I firmly believe, now, that the truly great athlete is so uniquely gifted that he has the ability to react purely instinctively while most of us are in the process of **thinking** about what to do. More often than not, the gifted athlete is a relatively poor teacher. His natural talents have been so great as to preclude the necessity for him to become analytical about the game he plays, or what he actually does when he plays it.

On the other hand, being a marginal athlete, as I am, requires that I search out ways and means to compensate for my athletic ineptitudes if I am going to have any chance to play competitively. It is in this spirit that I offer this discussion for you to explore. It is written out of a love for the game's physical and mental challenges, and dedicated to those who have a desire to explore its intricacies. It is with the recognition that there are very few exceptionally gifted, instinctive athletes out there on the racquetball courts. There are many, many more players of average ability who have a strong desire to get the most out of what they have.

I would like to express my deep appreciation to Gene Lenz for two things: first for being the influence that started me thinking about racquetball strategy; and second for providing me with the occasional opportunity to play with someone older than I.

Victor I. Spear, M.D.
October 19, 1976

THE BASIC
WINNING STRATEGY

Throughout this book I will be moving from one extreme to the other. I will attempt to simplify some things while meticulously complicating others, consolidating some subjects while expanding others, reducing the options on some situations while increasing them on others. But one theme must pervade every aspect of the game:

Hit a dead winner every time you have a good opportunity. If you can't hit a dead winner, hit a perfect defensive shot. Never hit anything in between.

If you take nothing else from this book, let it be this concept. Either put a quick end to the point with your next shot, or put your opponent in the worst possible position to do the same. The half-hearted, chest-high, slam-the-ball-around, "in-between" shots make the difference between the poor player and the good one. Don't feel too badly about hitting a poor kill shot or passing shot if you have chosen the correct, high percentage shot. You ought to feel much worse about your performance when you choose the **wrong** shot in a critical situation.

You may have no more than a split second to decide whether to go for a winner or a defensive shot (which, in most cases, will be a ceiling shot to the left corner), but you have to discipline yourself to act decisively. Don't hit compromise shots unless you want to commit racquetball suicide.

What is a "correct" shot? What is an "incorrect" shot? That's what this book is all about. Its purpose is to help you choose smart shots; to help you train yourself to eliminate the stupid and meaningless shots from your game. Study and analysis will never give you execution skills that you are not otherwise capable of. But study and analysis may permit you to better discipline yourself to choose the shots which keep all the odds on your side.

For the sake of simplicity, in the discussions which follow, it will be assumed that two right-handed players are competing. Hence, the left court is always the backhand court. If you are left-handed, or planning a strategy against a left-handed opponent, make the necessary transpositions as you go along.

chapter i

Serving to Win

Because the game of racquetball so rarely lends itself to service aces (as in tennis), the serve is often discounted as being unimportant. It is approached by many players as no more than a trivial necessity to get the ball into play (as in badminton or volleyball.) This exhibits a gross misunderstanding of the situation, and misses the vital point:

The purpose of a good serve is <u>not</u> to win the point with an ace, but to create enough difficulty to force a weak return, so as to win the point on the <u>second</u> shot.

There is also another thing to consider. Many players consider the serve return an ideal kill shot opportunity because they have so much time to set up properly. They may hit kill shots on 50% or more opportunities regardless of what kind of serve is offered up. In order to reduce the effectiveness of their execution, the serve must be carefully placed. So you may want to look at serving another way:

It isn't so much a matter of hitting <u>good</u> serves as it is to <u>avoid</u> hitting <u>poor</u> ones that might result in kill shot set-ups.

There is simply no excuse for not serving well, because:

1. You are rested.
2. You have plenty of time to think.
3. You are never rushed.
4. You know what you are going to do before he does.
5. You have many more options than you might realize.
6. You have a guaranteed positional advantage.

The key to effective serving is **variety.** This may seem simplistic, but you must recognize that no matter how well-placed a serve may be, a good player will adapt to it in time. In order to make every serve a challenge, there must be a mind-boggling mixture, so that he never has a chance to adjust to anything. The player who repeatedly hits nothing but low drives to the left corner may execute that particular serve well, but his effectiveness will diminish as the game goes on, and his opponent becomes grooved in the right tempo. The value of all serves can be increased many times by mixing them up.

If I began by saying that there are twenty different serves in racquetball, you might at first think you had read a misprint. Think again. There may be no more than three or four basic serve **types,** but each of these can be tremendously influenced by such factors as:

1. The server's court position (angle)
2. The sharpness and speed of the stroke

3. The height of the ball
4. The court depth of the shot

When you re-appraise the serve with these variables in mind, you begin to get the message:

There may actually be as many as one hundred serves in racquetball!

The most important serves will be described briefly, with or without comment, and accompanied by a diagram. Keep in mind, however, that the subtle differences resulting from variations in speed, height and server's position cannot be clearly illustrated by the diagrams.

THE MAJOR SERVES
OF RACQUETBALL

1. Low drive to the left corner from center court.

   This serve should be hit low and sharply, so as to barely reach the back wall crotch before the second bounce. If the serve carries too deeply and comes up off the back wall, it may be a kill shot opportunity for a good shooter. If your opponent tends to move up on this one, angle it more widely, so as to hit the side wall before he gets to it. (Diag. 1)

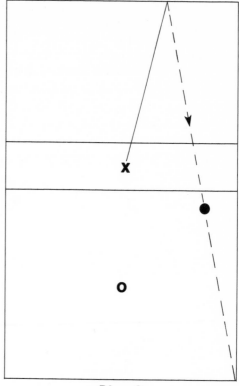

Diag. 2
Serve #2

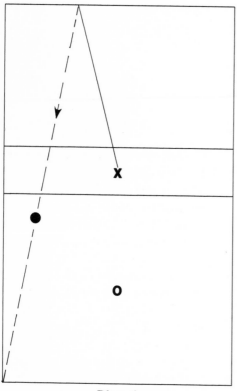

Diag. 1
Serve #1

2. Low drive to the right corner from center court.

   Same comments as for serve #1. (Diag. 2)

3. Low drive to the left corner from right-center court.

   The depth should be the same as in #1. This serve is angled more sharply away from the player, and can be very effective against a tired player in the late stages of a match. It is also more demanding on the server, as it requires a quick move to the left side after serving (described at the end of this chapter.)

4. Low drive to the right corner from left-center court.

   Same comments as for serve #3.

5. Lob serve to the left corner from center court.

This serve is designed to hit the side wall deep in the back court, so as to rebound falling to the back wall with nothing left on it. It requires a very delicate touch with superior accuracy. The margin of error is very slim, compared to the above. If it's just a fraction off, it can be transformed from a difficult serve to an easy set-up. This is one serve to be abandoned if you are having trouble with accurate placement. (Diag. 3)

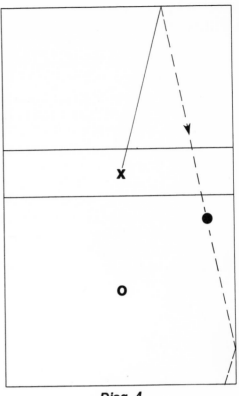

Diag. 4
Serve #6

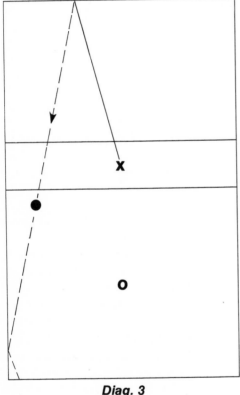

Diag. 3
Serve #5

6. Lob serve to the right corner from center court.

Same comments as for serve #5. (Diag. 4)

7. "Short corner" serve to the left from center or right center court.

This is, of course, a misnomer, because the target is not actually a corner. The "corner" refers to the angle made by the short line and the side wall crotch. This is one of the rare examples of trying to get the serve in for a quick ace. It is a low driving serve designed to almost "crack out" just barely over the service line. To have any hope of success on this serve, the ball must be struck at a very low point, just above the floor. The margin of error is small here, but if you miss, you are better off missing **short,** thereby getting a second chance to serve. If you miss long or high, the ball comes back to the center for an easy set-up.

This serve can be a game winner against a tired player at the end of a match. (Diag. 5)

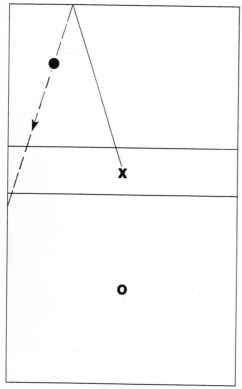

Diag. 5
Serve #7

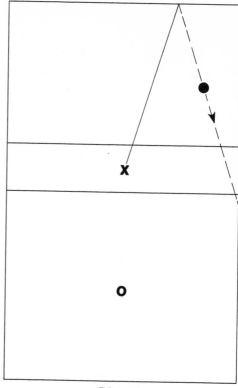

Diag. 6
Serve #8

8. "Short corner" serve to the right from center or left center court.

Same comments as for serve #7. The short corner serve to the right can also be very effective from **right** center court, but a good referee will call a screen on the serve, or at least he should. (Diag. 6)

9. Z-serve to the left corner from left center court.

This serve should be hit low and sharply so as to reach the side wall deep into the back court about waist high, and die into the back wall with a lot of down spin. The key to this serve is the depth of the side wall contact. If it comes in shallow, the receiver can move up and hit a cross-court pass. If it comes in too deep and rebounds off the back wall, it may be a set-up kill shot for a good shooter. (Diag. 7)

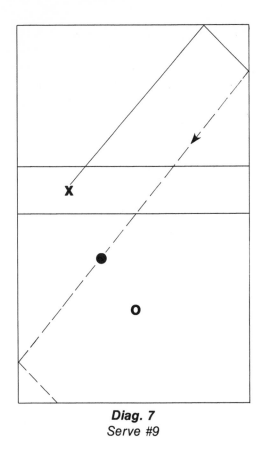

Diag. 7
Serve #9

Diag. 8
Serve #10

10. Z-serve to the right corner from right center court.

    Same comments as for serve #9. This can be a surprisingly effective serve if consistently well-placed against a player who isn't accustomed to it, even if he is a good forehand shooter. (Diag. 8)

11. Z-serve half-lob to the left corner from left center court.

    This serve varies from #9 in three ways. It should be delivered less sharply, slightly higher and angled more directly into the back corner with nothing left on it after it hits. This serve is the safest, most reliable and least risky of any to use as a **second serve.** If executed properly, it eliminates

everything but a ceiling shot return.

12. Z-serve half-lob to the right corner from right center court.

    Same comments as for serve #11, but more risky, and not as good for a second serve.

13. Z-serve to the left corner from **right** center court.

    This is a serve that is seldom used by most players, so it may have some intrinsic value as a secret weapon of sorts. It should be angled so as to hit the back wall before the side wall. Because of the unusual service position, it can come off the back wall with a very surprising type of spin, causing it to jump straight forward and forcing the unwitting player into a weak return. **This serve is** most effective when mixed in with the other more commonly used varieties of Z-serves to the left corner. (Diag. 9)

14. Z-serve to the right corner from **left** center court.
    Same comments as for serve #13, but more risky. (Diag. 10)

15. High bounce overhead Z-serve to left corner from left center court.
    This serve can be delivered in various ways so as to hit either side wall or back wall first and give rise to unusual spins. At times it may come off the side wall directly parallel with the back wall, as an ideal Z-ball does in regular play. (The only reply to this, of course, is to cut it off short before it hits the side wall.)

16. High bounce overhead Z-serve to right corner from right center court.
    Same comments as for serve #15.

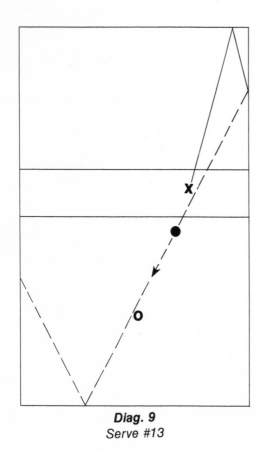

Diag. 9
Serve #13

Diag. 10
Serve #14

17. "Wallpaper" serve to the left corner from the left edge.

   This serve is delivered as a soft high lob which just barely misses the left wall throughout its entire course. Some players can drive you nuts with this serve, but it is very difficult to execute, and there is always the danger of hitting the side wall before the front wall which results in loss of serve. (Diag. 11)

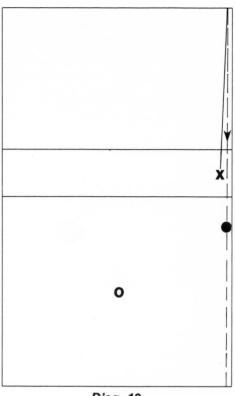

Diag. 12
Serve #18

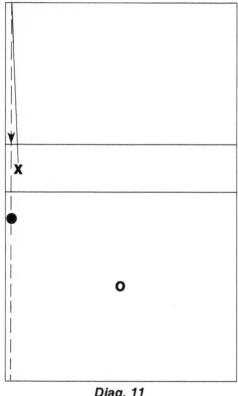

Diag. 11
Serve #17

18. "Wallpaper" serve to right corner from the right edge.

   Same comments as for serve #17, but probably best saved to use against a left-handed player. (Diag. 12)

19. "Garbage" serve to the left from center court.

   This is a lob serve without the high arc. It is delivered very softly at about shoulder height, so as to bounce about four feet past the service line, and then reach the back wall in a softly descending arc. Corner direction is not crucial. Its primary purpose is to prevent a kill shot return. If served correctly, there is never an opportunity for the receiver to strike the ball below the waist. A ceiling shot return can be expected.

20. "Garbage" serve to the right from center court.

   Same comments as for serve #19, but more dangerous if depth is not perfect.

There is an almost infinite variety of serve possibilities based on subtle changes in speed, height, angle and serving position. Keep an open mind to other possibilities, and don't be afraid to try a new one once in a while.

GENERAL COMMENTS ON SERVING

1. **Every** serve should be delivered with full concentration in an effort to draw a poor return, winning the point on the next shot. Good serves also allow very few point-stealing kill shots on the return.

2. The importance of having a **right-side serving game** to augment the usual left-corner serves cannot be overemphasized. Consider the following:

   a. The greater the variety, the more difficult each serve becomes.

   b. The player never has a chance to become grooved on the tempo of any serve.

   c. The player is probably not accustomed to very many right-side serves. (Watch the forehand kill shot specialist fall over in a state of shock when you begin serving to the right side!)

   d. You will occasionally uncover a glaring weakness in his returns

on one of these serves (i.e. the Z-serve to the right corner.)

   e. The short corner serve to the right is very effective against a tired player near the end of a long match.

   f. You must have these serves in your bag, anyway, to use against a left-handed opponent.

3. It must be conceded that right-side serves are more risky, being delivered, in general, to your opponent's strength. Greater accuracy is called for. You may get away with a minor error served to the left, but the same error on the right side is more likely to result in a quick loss of point.

4. Keep your opponent's most recent error in mind when you select your next serve. Most players tend to over-compensate for the error, and this human tendency can be capitalized to your advantage. For example, if he has just made an error in judgment by allowing a Z-serve to the left to die at his feet off the back wall by not moving up and hitting the ball soon enough, he is likely to move up on the next one. Why not sharpen the angle on the same serve so as to hit the side-wall further forward, and jam him from his intent?

5. You haven't truly completed the act of serving until you have made your first move toward your next position to anticipate his return. Discipline yourself to think of this **before** serving. Don't leave yourself open to simple pot shots and painful surprises. This leads us to the next subject.

POSITION AFTER SERVING

Center court position is so rigidly adhered to by most mediocre racquetball players that it easily ranks as the single most common positional **error** of the game. It arises out of a naive conclusion that center court represents the best spot from which you can cover all other areas. This line of thinking would certainly hold true if balls were merely dropping from the heavens, at random. But the balls are coming from the corners 99% of the time, so you must adjust your position accordingly.

When the serve has been properly delivered to the left corner, the correct position should then be:

One full step to the left of center, just behind the service line. (Diag. 13)

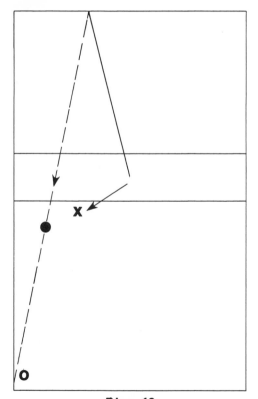

Diag. 13
Position after serve to left corner

The rationale to support the off-center position is made up of the following points:

1. It gives you an extra step to retrieve an attempted same-side kill shot return.
2. It guards against an attempted down-the-wall passing shot.
3. Most important of all, it almost eliminates the possibility of a cross-court passing shot, because your body is in the way. This only applies, however, to a well-placed serve. If the serve comes in too short, he can move up and still hit a cross-court pass by you (which further illustrates the importance of accurate serve placements.)

It may be argued that by taking the off-center position, you leave the long diagonal open, and allow him to hit a kill shot to the opposite corner. So be it. It's a good trade. You are inviting him to execute a very difficult, low percentage shot, while at the same time robbing him of his bread-and-butter shot.

Once you have served and moved toward your destination, you are still not finished. There are two more jobs to do:

1. Watch the ball until the actual contact is made, so as to gain some inkling as to where the return is going. This is also important in order to observe where your serve actually ends up, so as to make necessary adjustments in depth as you go along. In fact, you should never take your eye off the ball.

You don't have to stand still to watch the ball. You can be moving all the time. Players who serve and turn their backs on the ball can be punished for their sins in a variety of obvious ways.

2. Watch the position of the feet and legs. If you get into the habit of doing this, you will begin to pick up clues as to whether the player is going to kill the ball, hit a cross-court pass or go to the ceiling. For example, many players will bend the knees and lean into the shot more when they are about to hit a kill shot. This type of observation can give you a full step headstart towards retrieving an otherwise winning return.

All of the above applies, of course, to right side serves:

Take a position one full step to the right of center just behind the service line. (Diag. 14)

A common error that you will often see is a player serving a low drive from left-center court to the right corner, and failing to move to the right. Answer: He should be burned with a low forehand pass down the wall.

Another error, perhaps more common, is fading back to 3/4 court depth immediately after serving. This often occurs late in the match, when legs and brain are getting tired. In this position, the server is highly vulnerable to the quick kill shot return.

Diag. 14
Position after serve to right corner

chapter ii

The Strategy of Returning Serve

There is no question that this shot is **the most important shot in the game.** When two evenly matched players tangle, the outcome will usually depend on which player returns more serves poorly. Whenever you find yourself losing several points in a streak, in a relatively few minutes, it is probably the result of hitting weak serve returns, allowing the server to burn you with easy kill shots on his second shot. Remember that this is the only time in the game when your opponent has an automatic positional advantage: center court control, with you three steps behind in the back court. If you can't get the server out of the driver's seat, you are going to lose. If you give him anything decent to hit in his area of influence, you are going to lose. Watch a few other games and you will soon see that the player who is behind is the one who isn't returning serve well enough to move the server back into the corner.

If you want to select one part of the game to initiate your improvement efforts, this is it. Concentrate on returning serve above all else, and see how your results improve.

After hammering forth on the idea of variety in serve selection, I'm going to do a flip-flop on this issue. I would recommend the opposite approach to this problem: **use a minimum of different serve returns.**

If you can correctly execute three basic serve returns with consistency, you have little need for any more variety. Other options will be discussed only for the purpose of taking care of special situations and for completeness.

The cardinal rule of returning serve is the same as the basic strategy of racquetball:

Either try to hit a dead winner, or else as perfect a defensive shot as possible — but nothing in between.

Either hit a shot (kill or pass) which will quickly and conclusively put an end to the point before he even touches the ball again, or hit a defensive shot which allows you to **change positions with the server.**

THE THREE MOST
IMPORTANT SERVE RETURNS

1. **Ceiling shot to the left corner.**

This should be the mainstay of your serve return game. It gives you the best opportunity to force the server into the back court. Against a poor server, you can get aggressive more often with kill shots and passing shots. A good player will not give you many chances to hit a dead winner off the serve, so the burden is transferred to you to prevent him from having the dead winner on the next shot.

A properly executed ceiling shot, dying in the left corner, leaves the server the least possible opportunity to go for a winner on his second shot. He is forced to hit a chest high backhand scrape off the left wall, and if he doesn't, he isn't going to be able to hit it at all after it drops. He will usually return another ceiling shot, but this may be difficult to place if he is driven well back into the corner.

It requires a lot of skill and practice to place this shot accurately. The most common pitfalls are:

a. If the ball hits the front wall too close to the corner, it will catch the side wall on the way back, rebounding toward the center at mid-court for an easy set-up.

b. If it is hit too softly, it won't make it past 3/4 court depth and can be jumped on for a kill or pass.

c. If it is hit too strongly, it rebounds too far forward off the back wall, a set-up that many kill shot artists eat for break-fast. On a super-live court, it can be difficult to hit a super-live ball softly enough to keep it off the back wall. One remedy for this is to hit the front wall **before** the ceiling, instead of the usual reverse. This will take a lot off of the ball, and may permit you to regulate the depth with more control. This may be implemented from most areas on the court, but is almost impossible to hit correctly from deep in the back court. The only other situation in which the front-wall-first ceiling shot is indicated is on a front-wall-trap. (See page 48). In all other instances the ball should hit the ceiling **before** the front wall.

d. If it hits the ceiling too close to the front wall crotch, it plops down in mid-court without enough overspin to carry it to the back wall; another easy set-up.

e. If it is too far away from the corner, it will come back for a much easier forehand return. This is the most common error in the ceiling game, and it occurs as a result of pure care-lessness. Most players simply don't put forth the interest or the effort to get the most mile-age out of this shot. They seem to feel quite satisfied with them-selves if the shot merely achieves the short-sighted objective of driving the opponent some-where into the backcourt. **This**

is not good enough. If you have enough time to hit a ceiling shot, you also have enough time to hit it well. Why not give him a difficult shot to return?

Concentrate on hitting **every** ceiling shot to perfection and you might be surprised at how many "accidental" winners you get. A perfectly executed ceiling shot which wallpapers itself into the left corner can turn out a point winner just as big as a roll out kill shot, and it's ten times more frustrating to your opponent. It is also the only shot in the game that can cause a good player to whiff.

2. **Kill shot down the wall (near corner)**

This is the quickest, most definitive way to punish a poor serve. No one should dictate as to how often this shot should be tried. It can't be reduced to percentages because it depends on too many variables:

a. How poor the serve is

    You may choose this return as often as 50% of the time if serves are set up as pumpkins.

b. Where the server moves after he serves

    This shot is usually called for in response to a server who fades back like a quarterback to 3/4 court depth.

c. The score in the game

    I don't recommend this shot when you are facing match point, unless you have a lot more guts than I do, and a better kill shot.

d. How well you generally hit this shot

    Individual strengths and weaknesses must always be taken into account. Don't ever force yourself to do something in which you have no confidence, regardless of what any book says.

e. How tired you are

    When you reach a point of critical exhaustion, you should choose this shot more often. After all, your energy resource will get progressively worse as the point goes on. You might as well go for broke before you start wheezing.

f. How good your ceiling game is

    You may execute ceiling shots so well that you never have need to hit a kill shot from back court. That's the beauty of a strong ceiling game: it gives rise to so many kill shot opportunities in mid-court that you don't have to be a great back court shooter to win.

In summary, consider this: hitting a kill shot on a serve return is a risky situation. It must be executed with even more precision than an average kill shot because you are catering to a positional advantage when you hit it. Your position is the very worst, while your opponent, if he is paying attention, has the very best. If the shot comes up a little high, he has you at his mercy and can beat you several ways. Your margin of error is very slim. Either bury it low, low in the corner, or you'd better hit a different shot. Choose your spots well.

3. Cross-court passing shot

This shot is a necessary partner to the kill shot, both tactically and psychologically. It must be mixed in with kill shot returns in order to prevent the server from getting the forward jump on your kill shot attempts. You must keep him honest or he will virtually nullify your kill shot returns by charging toward the left corner every time he hits a poor serve. You must choose the cross court passing shot just often enough so that he is never quite sure what you are going to hit. The pitfalls are fairly obvious:

a. If the shot is not angled widely enough you are hopelessly vulnerable to the quick cut-off forehand kill to the right corner, plucked right out of the air.

b. If hit too high and hard, it can be retrieved off the back wall.

c. If angled too sharply into the corner, it hits the side wall too soon and rebounds back in toward center for an easy set-up.

The very best chance to execute this serve return to your advantage is against a serve that comes in too shallow. If you can strike the ball somewhere in the area between the service line and 3/4 court depth, you have the best possible angle to hit it by him on the other side.

It should be pointed out that a good player will rarely give you the opportunity to even hit this shot. If the serve is well placed in the left corner, and if he takes the correct position to the left of center, the angle necessary for the path of the ball is blocked out by his body. And it's legal, too.

OTHER LESS IMPORTANT RETURNS

4. Ceiling shot to the right corner

   This is a useful shot to hit when you are reaching for, and barely able to get to, a surprise low drive serve to the right corner. Instead of trying to hit a cross-court ceiling shot by reaching for it and hitting it across your body, hit a safer shot by staying on the right side with a ceiling shot down the wall to the right corner.

5. Cut-off shot (Hitting it before the bounce.)

   This is not only a good occasional option, but at times the **only** effective return against a good touch lob artist who stands there and gloats as you repeatedly fail to get your racquet on his soft, high lobs that die in the corner. That serve can give you screaming nightmares if it's hit just right. You can nullify its effectiveness by stepping up and hitting it on the fly, usually to the ceiling, but even as a kill shot or cross-court pass when the opportunity presents itself.

6. Passing shot down-the-wall (near side)

   This shot should never be used against a player who is in the correct position. It's simply not possible to get it by him unless he goes into an acute state of apoplexy. The only instance which calls for this shot is when the server commits the sin of drifting over to the opposite side of center (or simply stays there) after serving to one corner. You will observe this most frequently on right-corner serves delivered from the left of center. Some players never seem to move over to the right of center after the serve, and can be easily beaten with a low forehand pass down the right side.

   There is another situation that often leads to this opportunity on the other side. When a player has misdirected a serve intended for the left corner, he often realizes that the ball is going to rebound toward the center, and drifts over to the right to avoid being hit by your shot. Exterminate him accordingly: hit a low backhand pass down the left side.

7. Z-ball

   This can be a very good serve return on a ball that comes in shallow (i.e., short of 3/4 court depth) but is virtually impossible to hit correctly from the back court. It can also be used as a variant when you move up quickly to cut off a lob serve in the air, but it is more difficult to execute properly in this situation.

8. Opposite corner kill shot

   This is a very poor percentage shot from the back court and deserves no further discussion.

9. Lob return.

   This shot has been rendered obsolete by the live ball.

GENERAL COMMENTS ON SERVE RETURNS

1. **Never** decide in advance on what shot you will hit as a serve return. Your chances for good execution are drastically altered by the depth, angle, speed and height of the ball. Play the shot that can be played best. **Never** commit yourself mentally to hitting the ball before or after it hits the side wall, or before or after it hits the back wall until you actually can see **where** it will hit the wall. If you make up your mind before you see the shot, a smart player will carve you up. There is nothing I like better than to serve against a player who has obviously decided to move up on a Z-serve to the left corner, because he has been repeatedly jammed in the corner. I simply sharpen the angle of the Z so as to hit the side wall farther forward, and jam him again.

2. Don't play back too far to receive serve. Most players take a position close to the back wall in order to conserve energy in retrieving the usual corner serves. This leaves them vulnerable to the only possible service ace in racquetball, the **short corner serve** (see page 12). In baseball, the hitter is always taught to think "fastball". The rationale is that he can always slow down to hit the slow curve if that happens to be the pitch. But if he is thinking "slow curve", the fastball would be in the catcher's mitt before he had a chance to readjust. I think this is analogous to the racquetball player receiving serve. You should always think "short corner" serve, and play up half way to the service line. You have plenty of time to drift back and retrieve the more traditional serves with ease.

You have no chance to reach a well-placed low, sharp, short corner serve if you are lolling against the back wall. By taking a forward position to receive serve, you can easily nullify a potential service ace. (Diag. 15)

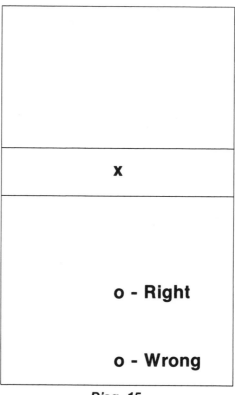

Diag. 15
Position to receive serve

3. Always take full advantage of the server's positional weaknesses. Punish the "faders" and the "drifters".

The "fader" is quickly identified as he serves and immediately takes three steps back as if he were Joe Namath. He has an unrealistic fear of being passed. Grant him his prayer. Don't pass him. Bury him with a kill shot return. It doesn't even have to be a very good one. There is no need to take the risk of trying to hit a roll out in this situation. A player who is running backwards has a very difficult time reversing direction to retrieve even a mediocre kill shot.

The "drifter" is the one who makes the lateral movement error going away from the ball. Burn him with a down-the-wall pass, as discussed on page 23.

4. Last, but not least, be ready to move up into better position immediately after attempting to hit a kill shot or pass. Don't just stand there and admire your shot. You are badly out of position for the reply if your shot turns out not to be a winner. Your only chance to get back into the point is to move up and try to anticipate his next shot. As you lean in to stroke the ball, you should already be in motion to follow your shot forward. You've already taken the first step; just keep moving.

If, on the other hand, you have chosen a ceiling shot return, you should have plenty of time to move up leisurely into a good position. But you still have to get there. Never assume that you will get a ceiling ball in return. Protect yourself against the possibility of an overhead kill shot.

chapter iii

Winning the Point

SHOOTING FOR A WINNER

The last two chapters have dealt primarily with the ways and means of extracting a weak shot from your opponent, whether on the serve return or later. Once you have achieved this objective, you **must** attempt to win the point with the next shot. You can't just stand there all day hitting ceiling balls, hoping that he will take a careless risk and hit one into the floor. If one of his returns comes back no further than mid-court, you must jump on the opportunity and hit a winner. You may never get another chance like that during the point. The next chance may be his. It is discouraging to watch a player work his heart out for eight or ten exchanges, finally get the weak return he's been looking for, and then **not take the shot.** He hits another ceiling shot and, inevitably, his opponent rolls out the next one. Don't let that happen. You can't always depend on your opponent to destroy himself. You have to beat him to win.

There are two primary winners in racquetball: the kill shot and the passing shot. Since the opportunity may call for a forehand or backhand, and the shot may go to the right or left, we arrive at eight possible shots that may be needed:

1. Forehand kill shot to the right corner
2. Forehand kill shot to the left corner
3. Forehand passing shot down the right side
4. Forehand passing shot down the left side (cross-court) (Diag. 16)

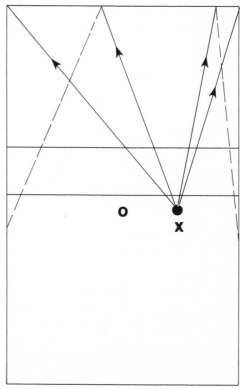

Diag. 16
Forehand winner options

5. Backhand kill shot to the right corner
6. Backhand kill shot to the left corner
7. Backhand passing shot down the right side (cross-court)
8. Backhand passing shot down the left side (Diag. 17)

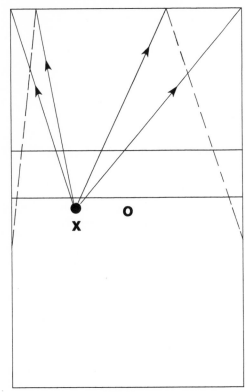

Diag. 17
Backhand winner options

These eight shots must be considered as separate entities, and worked on individually. It is mandatory to have each of these shots in your arsenal for two reasons:

1. Each opportunity you get favors the success of one shot over another. If you don't have the confidence to hit the obvious high percentage winner, you will have to resort to a shot with a lesser chance of doing the job.

2. If you are unable to hit winners all ways and from both sides, a smart player will quickly recognize your weaknesses, and simply keep the ball away from your strength. Worse, he will begin to anticipate your shot before you hit it, thereby gaining a critical one step advantage that may rob you of your best shot. You must keep him guessing.

If you are a player who can roll-out kill shots, don't bother with anything else, because the other player's position is irrelevant. But, if you are a player who, like most of us, hits many just-so-so kill shots, a little high and not exactly on target, you must be aware of one fact. These shots have no chance of being winners if your opponent is moving up on them before you strike the ball. And the only way you can prevent him from doing so, is to burn him with the cross-court passing shot as soon as he commits himself. The threat of the cross-court passing shot must always be in the air, and on his mind, to allow you to win with less than perfect kill shots. There has never been a good passing attack in football that lasted very long without the threat of a running attack hanging in the balance.

The reverse is also true. If, for example, your opponent realizes that you never hit a kill shot with your backhand (and he will, unless he has an IQ lower than the room temperature), you are in big trouble. Every time you get a set up on the left side, all he has to do is step back and protect himself from the cross-court pass.

How many players have you seen with outstanding backhand form who can retrieve beautifully, hit excellent ceiling shots, and good cross-court passes, but **never use the stroke to hit a kill shot?** These players may think they have strong backhands, but they are deluding themselves. They are backhand frauds. They have offensive games which are functioning only to 75% of capacity if they can't hit two of the eight major winners with consistency. You must be able to capitalize on a good opportunity by being definitive, not tentative, regardless of whether it occurs on your forehand or backhand side. This presents the game's biggest challenge to most players because their forehands are usually stronger. But face it: in the course of most matches there will be many more chances to hit backhand winners than forehand winners. It just doesn't seem that way, because so many players refuse to take the shot.

You should never walk off the court after a match without having hit every one of the listed eight winners **at least once.** Naturally, you will have your own particular favorites based on your skills, but the actual proportion of these shots in any given match should not be based on your pre-conceived choices. It should be the direct result of **which** opportunities are served up to you in that particular match. Or to put it another way: **you** don't decide how many kill shots or passing shots you hit, **he** does (by his position!) Certain positions of weakness almost seem to scream out for **one reply.**

Example. You serve to the left corner. He attempts a cross-court pass which is angled poorly and comes right back to your forehand, either directly or off the side wall. **You must hit a forehand kill to the right**

corner. His position and return demand it! No other shot has a better chance to win.

Example. You serve to the right corner. He attempts a cross-court pass to the left which fails and rebounds off the side wall to your backhand. **You must hit a backhand kill shot to the left corner.** His position and return demand it! No other shot has a better chance to win.

Example. You serve to the left corner. He attempts a kill shot to the left corner which comes up a little. You move up and **hit a backhand kill right back into the left corner.** A cross-court kill might also be considered because of his left side position, but in this instance your own position for execution of the shot would take precedence. In choosing a winner, you must always weigh the likely success of the shot against the relative difficulty of executing it.

This is the way you have to begin thinking if you are going to improve your game. You have to react in a flash, hitting the shot **most likely to succeed,** not your own personal favorite. And remember, these are eight totally different shots. Don't make the mistake of assuming that your ability to hit good forehand kill shots to the right corner automatically confers on you the blessing of equal skill in hitting the same shot to the left corner. The ability is there, but you may never have used the shot, and may not become skillful at it until you've hit it a few hundred times.

In summary, unless you develop the skill to hit kill shots and passing shots with uniform effectiveness from both sides and in both directions, you will not get the results your level of ability deserves. It is impossible to hit a passing shot for a winner when your opponent is hanging back at 3/4 court depth. It is equally impossible to hit most kill shots for winners when your opponent is creeping up ahead of the service line. It doesn't take a strategic genius to figure out that you should hit more kill shots when he is in the backcourt, and more passes when he is trapped up front.

WHEN TO GO FOR A WINNER

This is a question that can never have a concrete answer. There are too many relative variables. Two generalities can be made:

1. The lower you are able to strike the ball, the better chance you have to hit a winner.

2. The closer you are to the front wall, the better chance you have to hit a winner.

From this we can draw the following broad conclusion:

Anytime you have a chance to hit the ball knee-high or below from a court position anterior to 3/4 court depth, try to hit a winner. (Diag. 18)

As discussed in the previous section in detail, your choice of kill shot vs. passing shot, same side or cross-court, etc., is dictated by your opponent's position at the time.

You may, of course, also choose to hit a winner from the back court, off of a serve or a deep ceiling ball, but this should be an optional pick-and-choose situation used only in spots. It will be influenced by your level of fatigue, the score, his positional errors, how well you are executing your shots, etc. But don't lose perspective. Anyone who stands at the back wall and hits kill shots all day long is going to lose to a smart player.

Diag. 18
Winning area

KILL SHOTS

There will always be some debate on just where your target should be when you attempt a kill shot. I believe you should try to hit it dead into the corner. You will rarely achieve this. Most of the time it will result in a sidewall - front-wall (pinch shot) kill, or the reverse. Aiming directly into the corner allows for the greatest margin for error.

Your target should be 6-12 inches above the floor. The height of the target should be varied depending on your position on the court. You shouldn't aim quite as low on a kill shot from the back court, as you do on a set up in the service area. The odds won't allow it. Your opponent's position also influences the issue. You don't have to aim quite as low if he is burrowed in the back court, regardless of your own position. And lastly, the height of the target may have to be adjusted to fit the capability of the shooter. No one wants to stand there and hit half his kill shots into the floor.

As a general rule, hit your kill shots to the **near corner.** Forehand kill shots should be hit into the right corner 90% of the time. Backhand kills should be hit into the left corner 90% of the time. The earlier discussion of the "eight winning-shots" must not be misunderstood. It was not suggested that each of the eight shots be hit with the same frequency. It does enhance the value of your usual kill shot, however, to pop one over to the other side once in a while.

The cross-court kill shot is a more difficult shot to execute. First of all you are adding distance between you and the front wall by taking the diagonal. Second, you give up the advantage of the parallel side wall nearby to use as a guide to your shot path. In spite of all this, it's still wise to have the cross-court kill in your battery of shots to keep your opponent guessing, and for specific situations.

The best time to try this shot is when the ball is coming directly **from** the target area toward mid-court. If it comes all the way **across** court, on the other hand, you'd be better off to hit the kill shot down the wall into the natural near corner. But if it comes back to the middle, it can be quite difficult to change the direction of the ball 90 degrees to the other corner. In this instance it may be a better shot to kill it back into the same corner it came from.

> Example. A weak return rebounding from the left front corner to your forehand at mid-court: Hit a forehand kill right back into the left corner.

Two final points on kill shots:

Learn to hit all your kill shots with equal proficiency **before the bounce** as well as after. There are numerous opportunities when you can capitalize on his positional weakness by not waiting for the bounce. Particularly on a weak serve return, you can often pluck the ball out of the air with a quick flick cut-off kill shot before he even knows what happened, and has not yet dug himself out of the rear corner.

Secondly, don't get discouraged if you miss a few kill shots early in the game. Stay with the correct shot. You must not stop hitting the shot, or else your other shots will become less effective because of your opponent's anticipation. Most players try to take something off of the kill shot after they have missed a couple. I think the opposite is called for. **Hit it harder!** Early in the game your errors are often related to tension. The easiest way to relieve tension is with fierce action. So don't let up, hit it harder. Any baseball pitcher will tell you that it's easier to throw a strike with a fastball than with a slow pitch.

VARIATIONS OF KILL SHOTS

The phrase "a kill shot to the corner" is the way I have chosen to describe a particular attempt at hitting a winner. If we wish to dissect the game down to its finer points, we must then proceed a step further and subdivide this shot into three types:

1. Front wall kill - straight out
2. Front wall - side wall pinch shot
3. Side wall - front wall pinch shot
   (Diag. 19)

Your game would have to reach a high level of competence before it would be justifiable to spend time on these variations. For most players, I would strongly recommend that all this be ignored temporarily, to be taken up later. Just aim at the corner and let your shots end up as a random mixture of the above. But to those who have attained the enviable combination of shooting accuracy and quick thinking under fire, it is worth spending a few words on these variations.

It can't be denied that there are some advantages gained by the player who can add these variations to his kill shots. One such advantage is that he can angle the ball away from the other player who may be trapped on one side. The second

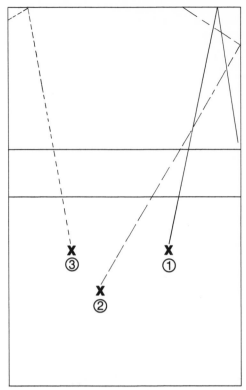

Diag. 19
Variations of kill shots
1. Straight out kill
2. Sidewall-frontwall pinch
3. Frontwall-sidewall pinch

advantage is that he need not hit bottom board on his kill shots. Hitting the second wall takes enough off the ball to bring it down some, so he doesn't have to take the risk of going for a roll out. He can get away with a kill shot that comes in slightly high if it hits two walls and is angled away from the other player.

It follows that a side wall-front wall kill shot should be chosen if you are shooting at the corner on the **same side** as the out-of-position opponent. It also follows that a front wall-side wall kill shot should be chosen if you are shooting at the **opposite side** of the out-of-position opponent.

It may be true that pinch shots are less risky insofar as skipping the ball in is concerned, because you don't have to aim so low. On the other side of the coin is the fact that it adds one more variable to the mathematics of the situation which makes it more difficult to execute. No smart basketball player deliberately tries to bank the ball in off the backboard on free throws. For most players, therefore, the straight-out kill shot should be preferred over the pinch shots in most situations.

These three variations may be kept in mind during solo practice on kill shot execution. But I think it is far more important to recognize the variations in the type of set-up you are trying to capitalize on. Here we find such a vast difference in execution that it is stretching the issue to even categorize them under the same heading.

KILL SHOT OPPORTUNITIES

When you practice kill shots, whether forehand or backhand, keep in mind that the kill shot opportunity arises from a wide variety of errors. The position, direction and action on the ball you have to hit will be quite different depending on the situation. Practice your kill shots by dividing your time between the following five types of set-up:

1. The ceiling shot that comes up short.

   This opportunity may result from three different errors:
   a. A shot that is hit too softly.
   b. A shot that hits too close to the ceiling crotch.
   c. A shot that is angled too close to the corner, and rebounds off the side wall.

   Take your time on this shot. You have all day to set up and wait for the drop. Hit the ball between knee and ankle height.

2. The ceiling shot that has been hit too deep, so as to rebound off the back wall at a good level.

   This is the most difficult of all kill shots to execute. It's also one of the most difficult shots in the game. The ball is dropping fast. It takes a perfect sense of timing combined with good footwork. To hit this shot well you must move forward with the flight of the ball so as to hit it **after** it is out in front of you. It must be hit off of your front foot. You can't just plant your feet and wait for the ball to come

to you. It is impossible to hit this shot unless it is well out in front. In addition, there is always the danger of misjudging the force of the ball in flight toward the back wall. If there isn't anything left on the ball, it hits the back wall and dies into the floor before you have a chance to get your racquet on it (the supreme ambition of every ceiling shot). You may, therefore, choose to hit another ceiling shot unless the ball is going over your head. Because of the surprising downspin the ceiling shot might have, it might be a safe compromise to follow a general rule of never allowing a ceiling shot to hit the back wall below the waist level.

3. The ceiling shot attempt, or passing shot, that misses the ceiling and rebounds strongly off of the back wall.

   This error usually results in an easy set up for a kill or pass. You will usually end up hitting this shot from a spot anterior to the service line. Always run forward with the flight of the ball and **wait for the ball to drop below knee level** before hitting your winner. In this situation, the drop shot (see page 37) may be added to your list of winning options. It may be the shot of choice, if he hangs back waiting for a pass. On the negative side, always be ready for the **front wall trap** (see page 48).

4. The kill shot attempt that comes up high.

The best choice in this situation is usually to re-kill the ball right back where it is coming from. Show your opponent exactly what his shot should have been, by better executing the same one he has just missed. That is doubly humiliating, like sticking the knife in and turning it twice.

5. A poor serve set-up.

Discussed in more detail in the last chapter.

The above five shot situations are so completely different that they must be practiced as separate kill shots in order to be ready for each opportunity as it appears. The skill on one shot does not automatically overlap onto another. I've seen many good shooters who execute the kill shot off a deep ceiling ball very poorly. They have the ability, as demonstrated on other kill shot opportunities, but they are too stubborn to practice this shot as a separate entity.

In summary, hit several kill shots from each of the above positions, with both backhand and forehand, when you practice. You might even arrange with a friend to practice killing serves, by each of you serving a wide variety of serves to be answered with a kill shot on every return.

PASSING SHOTS

(Some books discuss V-passes and cross-court passes as separate entities. Because I feel that the difference is merely one of geometric degree, I have elected to include both under the term "cross-court pass". The objective is clear: pass him on the other side.)

No instruction book can tell you exactly where to aim when you hit a passing shot. It is affected by your position on the court, and the position of the other player. You must, through practice, develop an instinctive feel for the proper rebound angles so as to barely outreach him. Sometimes it requires hitting the side wall to do so; sometimes it doesn't (hence, the "V-pass", "cross-court pass" division of terms.)

The most common error in this subject area, however, lies not in the angle but in the **height** of the shot. No matter how perfect your angle may be, the shot is absolutely worthless if it is hit too high. The player who should have been beaten is reborn. He merely follows the ball to the back wall, and gets another shot he doesn't deserve.

A good passing shot should never hit the back wall before the second bounce.

The target you aim for should be two to three feet above the floor. You may even want to go lower, so that the shot ends up simulating both a kill shot and a passing shot combined. In either case, it must be hit very sharply to have any chance of getting by the other player.

A cross-court passing shot must always be followed by an immediate move in that direction. Don't just stand there. You are highly vulnerable to a passing shot yourself if he manages to reach out and hit the ball before it gets by him. You must also be ready to make a quick move to the corner to retrieve a cut-off, down-the-wall kill shot which would be his best shot if the ball fails to pass him.

As a general rule, this shot should not be tried from deep in the back court unless the other player is badly out of position on one side of the court. In addition, a cross-court pass from the back corners is almost impossible to hit unless you make contact with the ball well out in front of you. Obviously, the passing shot is the most effective weapon when the opponent is both out of position **and** in the front court. This is when the familiar "hit-it-where-they-ain't" approach speaks for itself.

THE DROP SHOT

This shot is designed to "drop dead" very quickly after a soft tap to a low point on the front wall. It is a shot that once enjoyed a prominent and well-deserved place in the offensive strategy of the "old dead ball days." Since the new live ball became prevalent, if not universal, in 1971, this shot has been rendered almost obsolete. It is virtually impossible to hit a winner with this shot from the back court, or even mid-court unless the other player has fallen into a coma, so don't try it.

There are only two situations remaining in which the drop shot is not only useful, but may be the shot of choice:

1. When you are charging forward, **barely** able to retrieve a kill shot attempt just before it hits the floor for the second time, a quick-flick drop shot to the near corner is indicated. You are almost forced to go for a front court winner in a position like this, because you are so far out of the play. Anything your opponent is able to get his racquet on would probably beat you on the next shot.

2. On a shot rebounding off the back wall (usually a ceiling shot that missed the ceiling) far into the front court, run with the ball as it goes forward. Wait until the ball drops to knee level or below, and then take your choice. If the opponent follows you up there, pass him. If he hangs back for the passing shot, hit the drop shot. But never attempt the drop shot from above the knee. It is much too difficult to execute properly from that height. If the ball stays above the knee as you near the front wall, you

have entered a new situation, later designated **the front wall trap** (see page 48). Instead of having a set-up, you become the victim of a set-up. Never hit the drop shot from that position. Instead, go to the ceiling, and pray a lot.

Notice the similarities in the above situations. In both, you are being forced to make a shot in the front court, at least half way to the front wall. In both, you are moving forward as you hit the ball. The most common error in executing this shot is to hit it too hard and too high. This results from a failure to take into account the forward momentum of your charge, which adds force to the shot not being supplied by the stroke. It should be no more than a tap, with little or no wrist action used. (Diag. 20)

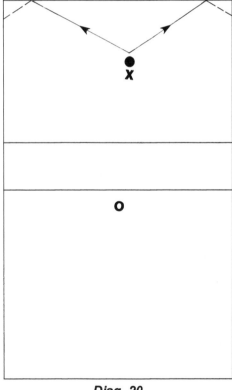

Diag. 20
Drop shot

THE CUT-OFF SHOT

This refers to any shot that you elect to hit **before** the first bounce. It contains some element of surprise and is particularly useful in three situations:

1. When your opponent attempts a passing shot serve return that fails to get by you, you may have an opportunity to pluck it out of the air on the fly and hit a quick kill shot down into the near corner. Take it! (Diag. 21) It may be true that this type of shot is more difficult to execute because you may be forced to hit it from above the knee, **but,** this is more than compensated for by the fact that he is far out of position, so you don't have to hit

a roll-out to have a winner. The player who lets this ball go by is sacrificing a golden chance for an easy point. Why allow the other player more time to move up into position? Why retreat to the back court to hit a longer shot, and at the same time, put yourself out of position? It takes very little practice to hit this shot almost as accurately as an ordinary kill shot off the floor.

2. When your opponent has been passed and manages to stay alive by hitting a diving, desperation shot **into** the back wall, don't let him stay alive for long. The shot will eventually come off the front wall with very little on it, usually in a soft, descending arc. You have plenty of time to see this all developing. Move up and hit it on the fly. This time you can wait for the ball to drop to the ideal level below the knee, and you have a variety of kill shots and drop shots at your disposal to annihilate him. Meanwhile, he is still trying to dig himself out of the back court, too late.

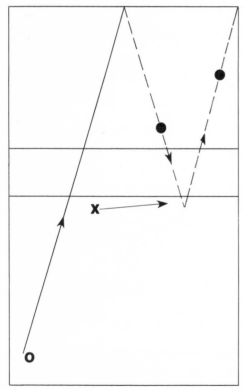

Diag. 21
Cut-off shot

3. Some players can drive you nuts with well placed lob serves. If a lob server is having a hot day, he can repeatedly serve up junk that you never seem to be able to get your racquet on for a full stroke. The only solution for this dilemma is to move up quickly, cut the ball off and hit it on the fly. You have the same three basic serve return options. You can go to the ceiling, hit a kill shot down into the near corner (if it drops low enough), or go for a cross-court pass. This is not a difficult move to execute. It

takes you out of the hole and, far more important, it disturbs the usual tempo of your opponent's game. This can prove to be very unnerving to a habitual lob server. Don't be surprised to see him go to a different serve, which he probably delivers less effectively.

One final point: Take care not to allow your forward motion to carry you into the service area until after you have hit the shot.

CEILING SHOT ALTERNATIVES

The beauty of a well placed ceiling shot is that it allows so few options. If it's perfect you have no choice but to return another ceiling shot. There will be times when you find yourself locked in a ceiling shot exchange that seems to go on forever. Be on the alert. A less-than-perfect ceiling shot return does, in fact, leave you with several alternatives, some of which can be point winners if your opponent has been lulled to sleep by the dullness of the rally. Consider the following:

1. Overhead forehand kill shot to the far corner.

   This shot is rarely, if ever, justified if your opponent is in the correct position on the court, one step behind the service line. It is worth an occasional try, however, against a mentally sluggish player hanging in the back court, looking up in the sky, waiting for the next ceiling shot to arrive. It is usually hit to the right corner because the other player is fixated back in the left rear corner where he received your last thirty-seven shots. This is a very difficult shot to pull off without a lot of practice. Any kill shot hit with a downward trajectory is difficult. Many players prefer to shoot this shot as a side-wall - frontwall pinch shot instead of going directly into the corner. In either case, the major problem is preventing the shot from coming up too high and being re-killed. And don't forget that **you** are also out of position as he charges up, hopefully too late, to retrieve the shot, so you must immediately make a move to follow your shot forward. Naturally, your chances of pulling this shot off will be greater if you are able to disguise your intention until the last possible instant before contact. (Diag. 22)

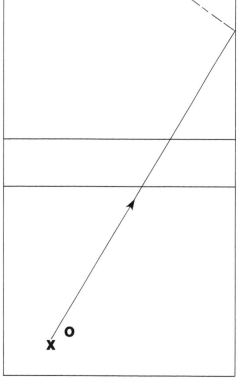

Diag. 22
Overhead kill

The same shot may be tried from the right rear corner to the left corner, but you won't have the opportunity very often, since most drawn-out ceiling shot exchanges occur on the left side.

2. Overhead forehand passing shot down the far side.

   Again, this shot will be successful

most often against a player out of position, begging to be punished. Accurate placement is very important on this shot, so that it does not result in a set-up if it doesn't go for a winner. Hit the front wall no more than three feet high so that the shot will bounce twice before hitting the back wall. Take care not to angle the shot in too close to the corner. If the ball catches the side wall on the way back, it's lights out! Follow the shot with an immediate move up the diagonal. (Diag. 23)

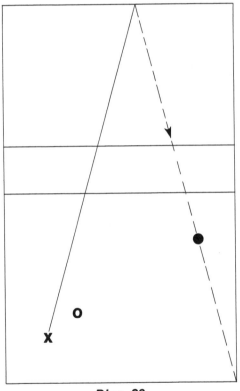

Diag. 23
Overhead pass

3. Cross-court ceiling shot to the other corner.

This is not a difficult shot, and is one you need to have in your bag to

use against a left-hander, anyway. I believe it should be tried more often. Most players have become so used to hitting ceiling shots from the left corner and back again that they have forgotten to test the opponent with a similar shot to the other side. It is true that the penalty may be more severe if the shot is hit poorly, because you give him a set-up in the area of his greatest strength. But an accurately placed ceiling shot presents just as many problems to the forehand as it does to the backhand. If he wants to come back to your backhand, he must play the angle perfectly, and he may just be a bit sloppy on this shot because he is so rarely tested on it. The most common error you will see is a return that is angled too sharply, rebounding off the side wall at mid-court for an easy set-up.

4. Z-ball

This shot is impossible to execute from deep in the back court, but it can be a useful and effective alternative on a ceiling shot return that can be struck at 3/4 court. Anything more shallow than that, of course, calls for an attempt at a more definitive winner.

5. Kill shot off the back wall

This shot is not possible, of course, on a perfect ceiling shot, which is supposed to die just above the back wall crotch. But it is inevitable after a long exchange that one of those ceiling shots will go deeper than intended. You then have an opportunity to put a quick end to the rally with a kill shot. This is a very difficult shot to execute, and requires a lot of practice. On the other hand, it need not be hit quite as low because the other player is usually lolling in the back court waiting for another ceiling shot.

6. Around-the-wall ball

This shot is driven high and cross-court such as a Z-ball, but it differs in that the target is the side wall **before** the front wall, instead of the reverse. The hope is that the ball then rebounds off the front wall across to the other side wall at about mid-court where it takes still another rebound into the opposite rear corner. If this shot is hit to perfection it can come off the third wall with a lot of downspin and be very difficult to hit. But there are too many variables of height and angle to contend with here. The number of set-ups resulting from this shot is too great to justify more than occasional use. A patient player can usually wait this one out and still have a relatively easy shot to hit. It might have some surprise value, however, against an inexperienced player. (Diag. 24)

All of the above alternatives to the ceiling shot can be, and must be, guarded against by moving up to the optimum position one step behind the service line after you hit every ceiling shot. It gets so monotonous, and seemingly wasteful, to run back and forth like that during a long ceiling shot exchange, that many players begin to cheat on themselves, and lag back. These are the opportunities to watch for — and capitalize on!

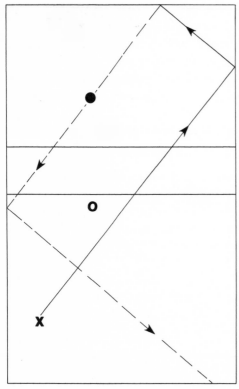

Diag. 24
Around-the-wall ball

BALL-WATCHING, FEET-WATCHING AND RACQUET-WATCHING

One of the trademarks and identifying characteristics of the racquetball beginner is his habit of serving and turning his back on the ball. He may even turn his back on any shot that goes into the back court during a rally. It's not that he wants to add mystery and surprise to the experience. His action is founded on the concern that if he watches the ball, he will become hypnotized and frozen into position, and consequently unable to react quickly to the next shot.

The accomplished player, on the other hand, never takes his eye off the ball at any time. He has trained himself to avoid the hypnotic fixation. He has learned to move with the flow of the ball at the same time he is watching it. You can train yourself to watch and move at the same time. It's worth a full step on any exchange, which could add up to a lot of points by the end of the match.

The highly skilled observer will also begin to recognize a pattern of characteristic feet positions as an indication to which shots are more likely to be hit. This is not something to be learned initially on the court in the heat of battle. It is best to go up into the gallery and watch a few players to get some idea of what to watch for. Then apply what you've learned to the action situations. Some players consistently tip off their kill shots with body language and feet position. You may even be able to spot some of these clues while they are warming up. Watch for the player who bends the knees and leans into the shot in an exaggerated way every time he hits a backhand kill shot, for example. Watch for the player who always signals a drop shot by taking an exaggerated backswing to try to throw you off. Watch for the player who takes a long stride into the ball when he hits a kill shot.

The racquet is one more thing to watch. Some players will cock the wrist noticeably more when they prepare to hit a backhand kill shot. Some players take a longer backswing on a forehand kill shot than they do on a passing shot. It may be of limited value to have such information on a set-up kill situation, but it is highly useful when he has his back to you, hitting a kill shot off of the back wall on a deep ceiling ball. You can just slip up ahead of the service line, and gobble up his "winner". There are few things more demoralizing to a player than hitting a good kill shot, and watching it being re-killed by a smarter player who had the jump on it.

These are some things you may be able to spot if you are looking for them. But you will never see them if thinking and observing do not become an integral part of your game. Why not accumulate every bit of available information possible during the course of scouting and playing? Each observation might be worth a point once in a while.

Have you seen any 21-20 games lately?

chapter iv

Special Situations

A complex game like racquetball does not lend itself to compartmentalization as well as many other games do. It turned out to be quite a chore for me to take a wide variety of thoughts and ideas, and turn them into an organized set of discussions under appropriate chapter headings. There are a few things that deserve some analysis that don't conveniently fit into any of the other chapters. This section touches on several unrelated special situations which have no connection with each other as you proceed from page to page.

THE (ALMOST) HOPELESS SITUATION MANEUVER

(What to do when your opponent has a set-up.)

You know that feeling you get when you've just attempted a kill shot which comes up high, and rebounds back to your opponent knee-high at mid-court?

You know that feeling you get when you've just attempted a routine ceiling shot which completely misses the ceiling, and rebounds off the back wall to the service area for a set-up?

You know that feeling you get when you've just attempted a ceiling shot to the left corner which hits the left wall at mid-court, and rebounds toward the center for a set-up?

What do you do? If you are like most players, you get angry with yourself, utter a few colorful words of disgust, and just stand there. This adds up to as much value as might be derived from leaving the court (which you probably also considered briefly.)

Why surrender? The ball is still in play, and as long as it remains in play, there is at least a glimmer of hope. Stop and think about it for a few seconds. Isn't there anything you can do, other than throwing a body block or praying for divine intervention, that might get you back into the point? I've been forced to analyze this situation because I've been in this position so many times.

Believe it or not, it's not completely hopeless. There is one and only one thing you can do, and **must** do:

Take away his best shot!

Just before he strikes the ball, make an all out charge toward the natural corner target of his kill shot, whether he sees you or not. Show yourself to him. Force him to try to make a perfect shot. Admittedly, you take yourself far out of position by this early move, but you have nothing to lose. He may pass you on the other side, and you are left standing there with egg on your face. But your position was hopeless, anyway. By making the premature move you might be saved three different ways:

1. You may be able to retrieve a kill shot that you never had a chance to reach otherwise.

2. You may intimidate your opponent to take his eye off the ball, and hit it into the floor as a direct result of your distracting move.

3. The cross-court pass, which is the correct shot against your premature move, may be hit too high, giving you a chance to save it off the back wall.

The above move at least gives you some chance in a position where you have none. At the very least, it's better than doing nothing at all. It's worth a try. What other options do you have? The next time your opponent is poised, licking his chops, for a set-up kill shot, make a sudden dash for his near corner. Then have a good chuckle as you watch him either blow the kill shot or hit a poor passing shot instead.

THE BACK WALL SAVE

When you have just been the victim of a well-executed passing shot, you have only one hope left — a lunge hit **into** the back wall with enough force to reach the front wall before the next bounce. The heads-up player will use this shot **only** in desperation, because the result will usually be another set-up for the opponent. The only thing accomplished is that it keeps you alive a few seconds longer. It forces your opponent to hit one more shot, leaving open the possibility that he might hit a poor one.

This shot should **never** be chosen if there is any chance of getting your racquet on the ball for a half decent shot directly forward to the front wall. It should be hit only as a last resort. One of the common errors seen in this regard is when a player with a poor backhand uses this shot on a good serve in the left corner, hitting a forehand stroke **into** the back wall. This is going to some extreme to avoid hitting a difficult backhand stroke. It makes the coach want to put his hands over his eyes.

THE EARLY FRONT WALL CHARGE

So many times throughout this discussion I have attempted to challenge the traditional "center-court control" concept, not by denying its essential rightness, but by pointing out and illustrating the exceptions to the rule. I would like to amplify this further in another connection.

We usually think of a kill shot as a shot that is chosen out of several alternatives. There are a few instances, however, when a kill shot is not a shot of choice but a shot of **necessity,** i.e., the only possible shot left for him to hit, a desperation shot.

Example. You've just hit a ceiling shot to the left corner. The shot is hit with almost perfect depth, but the other player elects **not** to hit it in the air, but waits to hit it off the back wall. When that ball hits the back wall, he will have no other option but to hit a kill shot just before it hits the floor.

Example. You've just executed a well placed Z-serve to the left corner which has hit the side wall and taken a nosedive toward the back wall with a lot of downspin. Because of the depth of the serve, your opponent would have been wise to hit this one **before** it hit the side wall, or, at least, **before** it hit the back wall, but he has done neither. After it hits the back wall, the only thing he has left is a desperation, scrape-the-floor kill shot.

Now, in each of these examples you have a split second to see what is developing. You know which shot he will hit before he hits it. One step behind the service line is no longer the best position.

Whenever your opponent is in big trouble in the back court, move up toward his near corner.

You have nothing to lose and everything to gain. By being alert, you have a two step jump to protect yourself against the desperation slop-shot kill. He has no chance of executing a cross-court pass from that position, so there is very little risk. And you just might save yourself the agony of losing a point to a lucky shot.

In summary, don't just stand there and admire a well-placed shot that gives your opponent trouble: move up and protect yourself against a low percentage, miracle return. It doesn't cost you any more than about two steps of effort. As a general rule, any ceiling ball that is allowed to go by without being hit in the air is most likely to result in a kill shot attempt off the back wall. As long as you know this, a forward position is clearly indicated, so as to give you a better chance to retrieve it, even if it is well executed.

THE FRONT WALL TRAP

When your opponent misses the ceiling on an attempted ceiling shot, the usual result is an easy set-up near the service area after the ball rebounds off the back wall. You will have several options to hit as winners, as discussed in Chapter III. Don't be overconfident.

Be on the alert for a trap.

If the rebound carries too strongly so as to drive you all the way up to the front wall, the entire situation may be reversed, and your opponent will end up with the set-up.

The critical difference is the height of the ball as you follow it forward. If it drops low enough to allow you the options of drop shot, kill shot or passing shot, your opponent has no chance. He must commit himself, and you can hit any of the three for a winner. But if the ball is still coming in high (above the knee) by the time you near the front wall, the drop shot and kill shot have been nullified, and he knows it. All he

has to do is to protect himself against the passing shot, and burn you on the next one. You are hopelessly out of position.

There is only one answer to the front wall trap. That is to recognize that your potentially offensive opportunity has been transformed to a defensive struggle for survival. Forget about your offensive options and **go to the ceiling,** and then run for your life to get back to center court. Sound familiar? It's a throwback to the basic strategy: if you can't hit a dead winner, hit a good defensive shot. Never attempt a drop shot on a ball you have to strike above the knee. Never hit a passing shot when you are out of position, and it is clear to your opponent that it can't be anything else. You simply have no good offensive choices in this dilemma. Incidentally, this ceiling shot must be hit in reverse order: the ball should hit the front wall first and then the ceiling, which would become painfully obvious the first time you tried to do it the other way from that position.

THE FRONTWALL-
BACKWALL-FRONTWALL
SHOT

SERENDIPITY: The faculty of making fortunate and unexpected discoveries by accident.

I have a "new" shot to discuss. I would like to say that I invented this shot by sheer intellect, but the truth of the matter is that I just stumbled over it by hitting a lot of bad shots. In golf, it is well known that the resulting position can be much worse after missing a shot just a little, than would be the case after missing it a lot. For example, the golfer may be better off after slicing a ball clear into the next fairway than he would be slicing it just as far as the trees and rough between the two fairways. This new tactic was derived out of hitting a terrible shot.

Almost invariably, when you miss the ceiling on an attempted ceiling shot, you've given your opponent a set-up. The ball rebounds off the back wall far up the court, he follows the ball forward until it drops to the ideal striking level, and then he snuffs you out any of six different ways.

Now follow this closely: If you hit a high, hard shot off the front wall close to the ceiling, but not touching it, the ball will come off the back wall with enough force to carry the other player **all the way** to the front wall without dropping below the waist. What began as an apparent set-up has turned into a trap. He is hopelessly out of position, and the ball is still too high to hit a kill shot or drop shot. His only hope is to go to the ceiling and try to re-group.

I don't recommend this shot as an integral part of your offensive strategy. It is not a shot you want to use very often. In fact, three times in a single match may be too often. There are too many variables to contend with, and the margin for error too great. But it certainly is worth an occasional try, for surprise effect, if nothing else.

I'd like to call it **The Spear Connection,** but if I did, someone would undoubtedly come up with some obscure publication revealing that Jim Thorpe or Abner Doubleday had introduced the shot a hundred years ago. I'm certain there are many players around the country who have stumbled over this shot accidentally, but never bothered to set it to print.

Try it. You might like it.

chapter v

Strategic Variations

If racquetball were like golf, there would be only one legitimate object of concern: yourself. Your shots would have no direct relationship to your opponent's shots. You would both be playing the same game, trying to shoot the low score. But golf is a solo game. At the moment of truth, when you make contact with the ball, you are alone in your own little world with that ball, and your opponent has nothing to do with it. You are virtually playing alone all of the time. You can plan your golf shots well in advance, so as to achieve the best possible score on every hole.

But racquetball is not like golf. It is an action-reaction sport. It is a four-wall chess game. Every move you make must be at least partially based on the previous move and current position of your opponent. If you bullheadedly plan your game too far ahead, and plow ahead with your preconceived ideas at all costs, while ignoring what your opponent is doing, you are going to be slaughtered. If you are unable to adapt your game to that of your opponent's strengths and weaknesses, you are going to find yourself losing, time and again, to players of lesser ability. Every move you make should be designed to cancel out his strengths and exaggerate yours, to cover up your weaknesses and magnify his.

When a player has a weak backhand, you'll be hitting more left side shots, and when he has a forehand weakness, you'll hit more right-side shots, etc. These are glaring, self-evident magnets that need no further discussion. But there is some value in discussing further the matter of **style.** The overall approach to the game varies so much from player to player, that individual shot weaknesses diminish in importance when compared to the total picture. I'd like to discuss two extremes in style, **the gunner** and **the rabbit.** If they have ability equal to yours, and you play the same game against both of them, you will most certainly lose to one or the other. If you'd like to beat them both, read on.

BEATING THE GUNNER

This is the guy who goes out on the court with one intention and one intention only — to shoot. At least half of his shots are attempted kill shots. Now if he is a terrible shooter with an ego problem, and just persists in hitting the ball into the floor, you have nothing to worry about. But if he is a good shooter who can roll them out with fairly good consistency, you have a considerable problem to cope with. What should you do?

The answer is clear: **shoot more,** i.e., go for more winners.

I find it very curious that few players reach this conclusion. The usual response to this kind of thinking is: "Why shoot more? I will only be playing **his** game." This is both superficial and erroneous analysis. You won't be playing his game at all. You will be **taking away** his game.

One of the most common strategic errors in the game is to try to play the move-the-ball-around, waiting game against the Gunner. This approach is suicidal. What you are waiting for is death. Don't be oblivious to the inevitable. The longer the rally goes on, the more likely it is that he will get his shot, and roll it out. For some unexplained reason, most players feel intimidated by a Gunner, and withdraw into a defensive shell. They are reluctant to shoot with him, when that is precisely the way to beat him. Try to hit as many early winners as possible, so that he has fewer opportunities to exercise his strength. You must take more aggressive chances against this player. You must kill more serves. There is nothing more deflating to a Gunner than to watch you hit a good kill shot serve return. You stop him from scoring before he even has one chance to shoot the ball. There is no way he can **serve** a kill shot.

The same strategy applies to playing anyone who is clearly better than you are. The longer the point goes on, the more likely he is going to win it. So why not shoot more? You wouldn't dispute the fact that your chances to win a five point game would be better than your chances in a full game. Doesn't the same reasoning apply to an individual rally?

I was faced one day with the dismal and potentially embarrassing prospect of playing an exhibition game against a professional who was in town giving a racquetball clinic. I thought about my chances, concluded that they were somewhere between zero and none, and realized that I had three choices: leave town, call in sick, or go out on the court and **shoot everything I could get my racquet on.** Naturally I chose the latter strategy and managed to get thirteen points, which was about ten more than I would have gotten with my usual methodical, waiting game.

Remember some of these thoughts the next time you come up head to head with your local champion, or draw the number one seed in a tournament.

BEATING THE RABBIT

This is the guy who gets to everything. This is the guy who has great agility and quick reflexes. The speed demon. The racehorse. This is the guy who reminds you of Charlie Hustle, charging all over the court, diving on the floor, crashing into walls, but always hitting your best shot back. This is the guy you have to beat three times to get one point.

But he is usually not a great shooter. He is basically a retriever. (If he is also a topnotch shooter, you'd better find someone else to play with.) Now if you try to go out and shoot against the Rabbit you are going to get killed. Half your kill shots he will save, and the other half you will hit into the floor, trying to hit it lower and lower so that he won't get to the ball.

The identical principle should be applied to the Rabbit as we did to the Gunner: take away his greatest strength. Since his strength is speed, play the type of game in which speed is not an asset.

This means throwing as many left corner ceiling shots at him as you possibly can, with a few Z-balls mixed in for variety. Hit winners only when he has been forced into a weak return that gives you such a good set-up that you can beat him three ways. It makes no sense at all to take high risk gambling shots against the Rabbit.

This strategy, designed to nullify his talents, will eventually frustrate him so much that he is likely to make some bad shots.

A final word on returning serve: It makes much more sense to hit kill shot serve returns against the Gunner than against the Rabbit. Trying to hit kill shot winners from the back court against a good Rabbit with center court position is certain to lead to your ruination. Unless you hit a roll-out, you will never get back into the point.

Summary: **Gun down the gunner.**
Bore the rabbit to death.

HOW TO TURN A LOSING
GAME AROUND

No matter how good a player you are, some days you are going to find yourself in the frustrating position of being far behind an opponent who is **not** a better player than you. How do you reverse this trend?

In tennis, the best coaches will always tell you to stay back if you are winning by staying back. But if you are losing with that strategy, you must rush the net more often. The same principle should apply to racquetball. Never argue with success, and don't be oblivious to failure. With the score 13-2 against you, you had better call a time out and think things over. But don't waste your time out. Use your thirty seconds to carefully and methodically plan specific changes in your game that might produce a turnaround.

1. Serving — If you have been concentrating on left side serves, try a few more to the right. If you have been hitting low drive serves, hit a few more lobs and off speed Z-serves.

2. Serve returns — This is the most likely source of your troubles. If you have been unable to control the ceiling shot to the left corner, try hitting a few to the right. If you have been hitting aggressive kill shot and passing shot returns without success, go back to a controlled ceiling game. If the reverse is true, try killing more serves.

3. Choice of winners — Some players are more easily beaten with kill shots than passing shots, and some the opposite. If necessary, change over to a predominance of one over

the other. If your kill shots are coming up high, or skipping in low, try a few cross-court kill shots. Just a small change in the angle can get you back on target again.

Now don't misunderstand the purpose of all this. I'm not suggesting that you spend weeks and months developing a sound racquetball strategy, and then go out and throw it all away just because you lose a few points. What I am trying to encourage is that you develop a versatility in your game which will allow you to change the tempo **temporarily** whenever necessary, in order to interrupt the momentum of a steamroller. No one can deny the value of momentum in an athletic struggle. Once you have recaptured this all-important force, you will be able to go back to your usual game with more favorable results. But you must do something to break up a long losing streak, even if it means hitting a few shots which are relatively unnatural to your style.

Nothing baffles me more than to watch a player losing point after point after point in exactly the same manner. **Stupid!** You may lose, but go out there with the attitude that your opponent will have to beat you ten different ways if he's going to beat you at all. In that case, you have lost to a better player, which is no disgrace. What really hurts is to lose to someone you should destroy.

Consider another possibility. It could be that you haven't sized up his game correctly. Perhaps the shots that make up your usual game play right into the strongest parts of his game. Unless you want to lose, you had better change your style for a while. You might discover, quite by accident, some glaring weaknesses in his game that you might never have found without exploring uncharted territory. I remember one match being completely reversed by simply changing to a right-side Z-serve which I found out (almost too late) that my opponent handled very poorly. Psychologically, it can be devastating. It's like having your pants pulled down in public in the fourth grade.

One final and very important point: No matter what aspects of your game you elect to change, the change must be highlighted by **more hustle.** This may seem unnecessary to point out, but it takes more effort than you might think. It goes completely contrary to your state of mind at the time. It is a very human tendency to let down some when you're losing badly. Most of us tend to run the least when we need to run the most. The only way to get out of a slump is to run harder. Dig after some of those kill shots that seem to be out of reach. You might surprise yourself and get to a few.

And what's more, running harder will help to ease the tension, which may have been the problem in the first place.

HOW TO WIN WHEN YOU'RE EXHAUSTED

I know that some of you readers out there are in my shoes — over 40, legs starting to give out (to say nothing of the lungs), endurance on the wane, speed no more than a distant memory. What is worse, we are frequently playing against an opponent fifteen years younger, faster, more durable, and invariably heartless and insulting, as he stays on the court to play another hour with someone else, while we stagger off to the intensive care unit, clutching a picture of George Blanda to our hearts.

Now it's one thing to sit down and plan a perfect racquetball strategy to guide us under normal conditions. The above, however, could hardly qualify as "normal". So it behooves us to develop a sub-strategy within the strategy, a **"Plan-B"** of sorts, to be unveiled when we can no longer execute according to theoretical guidelines. Perhaps you have your own set of warning signals, such as when your nailbeds begin turning blue, or when you stop sweating on one side of your body, or when you've just had to call time out with the score three to two, or when your wife leaves the gallery to call your insurance man, or when you begin to see palm trees and watery oases in front court.

All is not lost. With the application of a few minor adjustments, it is still possible to pull through.

1. This above all — **get your head together.** Guard against the common mental errors that you would never commit at any other time, such as fading or drifting after a serve, failing to move toward the ball after hitting a cross-court passing shot, etc. We generally think of fatigue as something that affects our shooting and running game. I think it is potentially more devastating to our **thinking game.** It is infinitely more difficult to concentrate when you are hang dog tired, but concentration becomes even more critical at such times. If you can't think straight, you might as well give up.

2. Be more careful not to serve up any pumpkins. Remember, it is not critical that you make a great serve, but you must avoid hitting poor ones.

3. Hit a kill shot serve return every good opportunity you get. You must change your usual percentages in this situation. Obviously, it is to your advantage to keep the rally as short as possible. What is more important is this: Your execution of shots will have a quality inversely proportional to your fatigue level. The very beginning of each point is the time when you have the most energy. So why not set yourself up and go for a winner as often as you can. The longer the rally goes on, the more likely you are to make an error.

4. Hit your forehand ceiling shots with an overspin stroke, similar to the way a tennis serve is hit, with a quarter-turned face. This will allow you to get the ball into the back court without swinging so hard. You may hit this shot with overspin normally, but if you don't, now is the time to do it.

5. Play an aggressive game. Don't make the mistake of trying to "pace yourself", so as to save something for the later stages. You'll never see the later stages. Go for every point. Try to make the game as short as possible, and you have a chance.

6. Don't cut corners on energy consumption by failing to set your feet properly before hitting a shot. One of the major flaws of a tired player is that he begins to hit backhand shots from a flat-foot position facing the front wall. You won't get away with this short-cut. Always make your full turn, facing the side wall, and stride into your backhand strokes.

7. Take the full ten seconds allotted to you by the rules between every point. It is stupid for a tired player to walk up and serve the ball immediately after winning a long rally. Stand there and take a few deep breaths. And **think.** Then serve.

BEATING THE TIRED PLAYER

After re-reading the previous segment for the first time, it occurred to me that I have always examined the issue from only one side, because I was always the tired player. But it's only fair to analyze the question from the point of view of the other player as well, painful though it may be. After all, you should get some reward for all the strenuous and boring hours of conditioning you have gone through to attain a higher level of endurance than your opponent. If this difference becomes more exaggerated as the match goes on, consider the following:

1. Serve the low drive, wide-angled serves to both corners, almost exclusively, with a few short-corner ace tries mixed in. He has much less time to react to a "no-wall" serve than to a Z-serve which hits three or four walls, or a lob serve which takes too long to get there.

2. On serve return, watch for the server to make the common error of fading back to 3/4 court depth. A tired player is much more likely to commit this mental mistake. When he does, he must be punished with a kill shot to the near corner. Don't take the risk of trying to hit bottom board in this situation. It isn't necessary. Hit a higher percentage, one-foot-high shot, and you will still win the point. He'll never get there, if he is moving backwards.

   If he doesn't make this mistake, don't hit kill shot returns.

3. Hit passing shots during the early part of a rally and then be ready to shift gears and hit a kill shot,

because he will fade back further and further as the rally goes on.

4. Move the ball around as much as possible. Standing in one spot trading ceiling shots with an exhausted player absolutely throws away all the built-in advantages you have.

5. Be ready to execute the ceiling shot alternatives (see page 40). The tired player is most vulnerable to lapses in concentration, and may not move back up into the correct position after every ceiling shot.

6. Dig extra hard on the long rallies to keep them going as long as possible. Every shot you can add to the exchange makes it more likely that your opponent will make an error on the next one.

7. Try an occasional hard, low drive directly at your opponent. This shot challenges a player more than it might appear at first glance. It requires a quick change of feet and body positions combined with quick thinking to choose the appropriate response. He is a sitting duck for this type of challenge.

8. Play good solid racquetball, above all. Don't be tempted to throw away all your well-disciplined principles of strategy just because your opponent is tired. You can't just pop the ball around and expect him to miss everything. Some players can reach a point of such exhaustion that they can barely move around, and still summon up enough desire to punish you for

your sins. So don't lose your total perspective. The above suggestions are merely adjuncts to the fundamental theories of racquetball strategy which should never be abandoned.

THE MASTER PSYCH

Mental and psychological factors can often prove to be highly significant in determining the outcome of an athletic struggle. It is neither dishonorable nor immoral to be aware of some of these factors, and to use them to your advantage. Watch Charlie Brumfield play a few times, and you will see a player whose raw talent is not greater than four or five other players on the pro tour. But he consistently overwhelms his opponents by his attitude, approach and superior understanding of the game. He knows exactly what to do, and when to do it, to take maximum advantage of his opponent's mental status.

Here are a few suggestions:

1. Pause for a minute or two during the warmup, and watch his feet. It may bother him some, and at the same time you will be learning about his body language.

2. If you lose the coin toss, try to hit a kill shot on his first serve, unless it is a very difficult one. Players rarely expect this, so it doesn't take a roll out to make a winner. If you succeed, you might rattle him. If not, it's only one point in a long game.

3. If he serves a lob, move up immediately and hit it before the bounce. This is very unnerving to most lob servers, and will enable you to take charge of the tempo of the game right away.

4. If you win the toss, try for an ace with a short corner serve. He is probably not ready for it. If you succeed, it's a great way to get off to a flying start. If you miss, you'd better be short, so that you don't give him a set-up.

5. Put out your greatest effort to win the longest rallies. The longer the point goes on, the harder you run. Nothing is more demoralizing to a player than to lose a point after he has played his heart out.

6. The second most demoralizing thing is to win one of those marathon rallies, and then to lose it all back on one shot. So if you lose one of those long ones, try hitting a kill shot against the very next serve, if at all possible. If you succeed, you will have delivered the greatest morale-buster in the game.

7. Dig extra hard on the first three or four points of the game. Most players tend to pace themselves early in the game, but you can gain a great plus for yourself in the early stages if you can manage to create the illusion that you are going to dig after, and are capable of getting to, **absolutely everything.** This can really shake your opponent up in a bad way. And it's also a good tension reliever for you. The more physical you can be right off, the sooner you attain that loose, relaxed fluidity that you need for good racquetball. All football players will tell you that they like to get in on the first tackle if they possibly can.

8. Call your time outs when they can be of advantage psychologically, as well as when you need them. Before serving match point in a close contest, a time out is worth a few shakes from your opponent's knees. I also enjoy calling time out when my opponent is upset about a referee's call. Why not let him stew about it a little longer? It might disturb his concentration.

? SHOULD STRATEGY DEPEND ON WHO HAS THE SERVE?

This is a question which is in constant debate in racquetball circles. The argument goes something like this: When you are serving, there is no actual risk of **losing points** on the scoreboard, so why not take more chances? When you are returning serve, every mistake is matched by a point on the scoreboard, so why take chances until you get the serve back? Doesn't this all make good sense?

No!

This shallow line of reasoning fails to recognize the very essence of the game. Your choices are dictated almost exclusively by the **position** of your opponent and his previous shot. Whoever served simply has nothing to do with the question. A smart shot is a smart shot, no matter who put the ball into play. A stupid shot is . . . , well, a rose is a rose is a rose.

I think the argument fails in another respect, as well. During a long, heated exchange rally, players who are concentrating on the problems at hand will eventually forget who served the ball. How many times can you recall standing there with your opponent during a practice game, trying to remember who started it all? The last thing you want to have on your mind at crucial turning points in a rally is to have to stop and think about who served, before you choose your next shot. This leads only to chaos and poor play. The whole purpose of developing a sound racquetball strategy is so that it will become so deeply integrated into your play that you begin to react instinctively. The long term goal is **less thinking,** not more.

Of course you will not take a low percentage kill shot opportunity when you are facing match point. That is simply good racquetball. That is a pick and choose situation. But if you get a **high** percentage kill shot set-up, you darn well better take the shot, even if the score is 0-20, because you probably won't get another one. You can't depend on the other player to oblige you by hitting one into the floor.

Those who argue this whole question somehow delude themselves into thinking that they can return serve, and then stand around hitting ceiling shots, *ad nauseum,* waiting for the other player to miss. Then, of course, they will have the serve, and go out and play aggressively. It's all a dream. They will never get the serve back. Smart players will beat them every time by simply waiting for the inevitable weak return, and burying the ball into the corner.

Obviously, you should be doing a lot more experimenting and feeling-out of your opponent during the early part of a match. You should, then, be ready for more definitive application, based upon what you have learned, in the late stages. But all is still within the framework of good, sound racquetball strategy. This must apply equally to both the serving and serve return positions.

So don't get trapped into simplistic thinking. **Play the right shots all the time.** The score will take care of itself.

chapter vi

Tournament Readiness

CONDITIONING

The most dangerous potential enemy to the smart racquetball player is **fatigue.** No matter how profound your understanding of the game, you cannot take advantage of your insight if you are too tired to apply it. No amount of theorizing will compensate for the disadvantages which result from poor conditioning. You cannot hit a kill shot properly if you don't have enough energy left to turn your body, set your feet and stride into the shot. You cannot hit a good ceiling shot if you don't have the strength to lift your arm above your head. You can't run, if you can't breathe.

The best conditioning for any sport is the sport itself. Nothing can simulate the actual muscular feats you will be called upon to perform quite so exactly as the game itself. If you are able, and willing, to play a strenuous game of racquetball for five or six hours every day against strong competition, don't bother to read the rest of this section. Inasmuch as most of us are unable, or choose not, to play that much, extra-curricular conditioning becomes mandatory.

Racquetball is a game of **hit and run.** I like to think of it as a threefold challenge to the arm, legs and lungs, and will approach the problem from those three aspects.

ARM TRAINING

A long match with a good defensive player who can execute ceiling shots well can sometimes wear you out to such an extent that you can't beat him even though you are the better player. He merely outlasts you. This can be prevented by a relatively simple program of exercises.

The shots of racquetball can be reduced to three basic motions: forehand, backhand and overhead. These motions can be almost exactly simulated and greatly strengthened by working with a weighted, hand pulley system such as you might find on the "universal gym" type apparatus, available at most Y.M.C.A.'s and health clubs. With the grip handle attached to the floor level pulley, the following three exercises are pertinent and right to the point.

1. Lie flat on your back, reaching with arm extended straight back to grasp the handle. Now pull forward until your arm is fully extended to your hip, and then back again (simulating an overhead stroke, against resistance.)

2. Stand sideways with your shooting arm next to the equipment, grasping the handle loosely at your side. Now pull the handle, with arm extended, all the way across your body in front of you, until you have reached shoulder height, and then back again (simulating a forehand stroke, against resistance.)

3. Turn 180° and stand sideways facing the opposite direction, loosely grasping the handle across your body in front of you near the opposite hip. Now pull the handle across your body and upward until your arm is fully extended, straight out sideways from your body, and back again (simulating a backhand stroke, against resistance.)

These exercises should be performed in a series of systematic increasing repetitions, and against a gradually increasing weight resistance. Don't push yourself too hard, at first, or you might end up with pulled muscles and strained tendons and ligaments.

The above series is directed primarily to strengthening the arm and shoulder, but it doesn't do much for the wrist. Supplement with a series of light weight wrist curls with a small bar bell for a stronger wrist action on your shots.

RUNNING

The debate over the relative value of sprints vs. long distance running will go on indefinitely. After having analyzed the issues both from the athletic and physiological points of view, I have come to a firm conclusion: Both sides are right, but neither to the exclusion of the other.

There is no denying the value of long distance running for the purpose of increasing endurance on the racquetball court. Both the collateral circulation of the vascular (heart and blood vessels) system, and the vital capacity of the pulmonary (lungs) system can be greatly enhanced by long distance running. In addition, the strengthening of the legs which must also occur, takes some of the burden off of the heart and lungs by virtue of greater efficiency. But long distance running does not simulate the game of racquetball, which is a game of starts and stops, sudden bursts of speed, followed by short rest periods, etc. Preparation for racquetball, therefore, requires that long distance running be supplemented by sessions devoted to highly irregular "slow jog - quick sprint - slow jog - quick sprint" type of workouts.

The best way to train for the racquetball season is to alternate each of the above on a regular daily basis. The exact distances and speeds must be tailored to fit the individual's capacity and previous training habits. Every program should be designed to increase the demands slowly and systematically according to the player's tolerance.

I would also recommend doing some running immediately before or after (or both) playing practice matches. This will help you to build your endurance

level even higher. You must push yourself at least a little bit beyond the level of tolerable fatigue if you are going to get anywhere. I'm reminded of the story about the runner who met his friend on the running track and asked him how far he planned to run. "Half a mile," was the reply. Observing that he was still running after thirty minutes, he approached him a second time. "I thought you said you came to run a half a mile?" The answer is a classic: "I did! I've already run four miles to warm up, but it's the **next** half mile that I really came to run!"

The message is clear. Unless you push yourself slightly beyond your previous endurance level, you never make any progress. You will be amazed how much further you can eventually run if you do it on a steady, planned, gradually increasing basis. I remember well the feeling of pride after having run two miles for the first time, never imagining that I would be able to raise that distance to seven miles within a year.

Two small things you can do during your practice matches might also help:

1. Never call timeouts when you get tired.

2. Dig for everything, including kill shots you know you can't reach.

Regarding the question of the best method of reaching your peak at tournament time, you will hear two opposing points of view. Some players feel that it is best to train vigorously right through the last day. Others advocate going easy the last couple of days. It isn't possible to generalize this issue. Each player is a unique physiologic entity, with differing energy levels and endurance patterns. Don't allow yourself to be talked into someone else's system. It never hurts to experiment once in a while on a trial basis, but if it doesn't feel right to you, go back to the system that makes you feel best.

TREATING THE ACHES

Racquetball easily qualifies as one of the most strenuous and physically demanding of any sport you can find. It is characterized by sudden starts and stops, twists and turns, dives and crashes, etc. I would like to interject here some medical advice on the sensible management of injuries and pain. This is probably the only section that I can claim to be perfectly qualified to write — not only because of my medical background, but because I'm hurting all the time from playing racquetball, and my wife has an aversion to whining.

The most common injury in racquetball is the sprain, usually the ankle or knee. This also happens to be the type of injury that most frequently receives the wrong first aid treatment. How many times have you seen an athlete on television sprain his ankle, and be immediately "attended to" with an icepack? I repeat: **wrong.** The icepack may be all right for a little later, but the very first move is the most important, and the very first move should be **pressure.** As soon as a sprain occurs, blood will begin to flow into the tissues from ruptured blood vessels, along with edema (watery) fluid from damaged cells. The resultant swelling can be held down as much as 90% if firm pressure is applied right away, and maintained. And you don't need any fancy gimmicks during the crucial, initial phase. Simply grab that ankle in a strangle-hold grip and hold it like a vice for ten minutes. Then wrap it firmly with an elastic bandage (Ace), but not so tight as to impair the circulation. These two steps will do more to prevent the swelling than a whole bucket of ice, which you can save for the large glass of scotch you will need at bedtime.

Over the course of the next few days, it may be necessary to keep it wrapped while you are hobbling about, in order to keep the swelling from recurring. But it isn't necessary to apply the pressure continuously. You may remove the elastic bandage at bedtime when you are ready to assume the horizontal position, but keep it at the bedside. The time to reapply it is **before you get out of bed** in the morning. The greatest amount of swelling occurs **immediately** after you take the upright position. So, if you get out of bed, stand at the mirror and shave for ten minutes, don't bother to put on the elastic bandage afterwards. It's already too late to prevent the swelling.

MUSCLE SORENESS

The most important factors in the prevention of muscle soreness are:

1. Good physical conditioning
2. Sensible warmup
3. Proper cooling down
4. Next day workout
5. Aspirin

THE WARM-UP

You will rarely see a professional athlete go out and start playing without a good warmup. This is even more essential in racquetball than it is in most other sports because of the physical demands made on the player. Never walk on the court without having gone through some exercise routine consisting primarily of stretch exercises and easy jogging. It need not take up more than ten or fifteen minutes, but it will go a long way toward prevention of muscle aches the next day. Needless to say, you will also play better.

Regardless of which combination of exercises you choose, certain general principles should be adhered to:

a. Start slowly
b. Gradually increase both the speed and the intensity of the exercises.
c. Try to include as many different muscle groups and joints as possible during the full course of your routine.
d. Combine muscle stretching with increased activity of the heart and lungs.

If you don't have your own set combination of warmup exercises, try the following twelve-minute routine on for size.

1. Slow jog — one minute

2. Arm circles — one minute

   Rotation of the outstretched arms alternately, through a full 360 degree rotation of the shoulder joint, first in a vertical plane, both forward and back, then in a horizontal plane, both forward and back. This is best done while walking.

3. Calf and hamstring stretcher — one minute

   Stand with one foot crossed over the other, with both feet flat on the floor. Slowly reach down to touch your toes without bending your knees. Repeat several times, and then cross over with the other foot and do the same.

4. Alternate toe touch from the standing position with gradually widening stance — one minute

5. Half-squats — one minute

   Starting with the upright position, slowly lower your body by bending your knees to the half-squat position with arms extended forward. Hold for three seconds, and repeat several times.

6. Jumping jacks — one minute

7. Medium jog — one minute

8. Knee-chest back stretchers — one minute

   Lying flat, hug both knees to your chest, and hold for three seconds. Extend, and repeat several times. (Most orthopedic surgeons caution against doing this exercise one knee at a time.)

9. Single leg raises — one minute

Lie on your back with hands folded under your head. Raise one leg up to the vertical position, and then back to the floor. Repeat several times, and then do the same with the other leg.

10. Hurdler's stretch — one minute

From a sitting position extend one leg backward at a 45 degree angle, bent at the knee. Then touch the forward foot with the same hand several times. Repeat with the legs reversed.

11. Fast jog — 2 minutes

If you have found the descriptions of any of these exercises difficult to comprehend, I would suggest *The Official Y.M.C.A. Physical Fitness Handbook* as a good source.

COOLING DOWN

After a strenuous match, muscles have a tendency to register their own form of silent protest at the abuse by tightening up. This may even progress to the point of painful spasms. This can be prevented, or at least significantly reduced, by a gradual tapering off of exercise, rather than going right from the court to the shower. **Standing still,** without support, which is the position I assume you would have in the shower, is the worst possible position to take immediately after a hard workout. It is far more physiologic, and less embarrassing to the musculo-skeletal system, to spend about ten minutes winding down. Alternate walking and jogging at a slow pace will do the job well. Once you have cooled down, sitting in a whirlpool or tub is far better than standing still in the shower. But if shower you must, then at least make it brief.

NEXT DAY WORKOUT

The most uncomfortable stiffness and soreness usually begins to set in about 24 hours later. This can be alleviated considerably by engaging in a short session of stretch exercises and light jogging sometime during the next day. This may be the last thing in the world you really feel like doing, but it's well worth it.

ASPIRIN

If all else fails you may have to resort to aspirin. Unfortunately, the familiar cliche, "Take two aspirins and call me in the morning," has blinded the American public to the real value of aspirin as a remedy for pain. Because it has become commonplace, this minor miracle rarely gets the recognition or appreciation it deserves. It is, without a doubt, the most underrated medication there is. But it is seldom used correctly. For maximum effectiveness, it should be taken as follows: two or three tablets every four hours around the clock (there is now available an eight-hour aspirin which can be used as the bedtime dose.) At times, it may even be necessary to begin the aspirin before playing, in order to establish effective blood levels. Don't wait until you start hurting. Regardless of how it is taken, three precautions must be noted:

1. Never take aspirin on an empty stomach. It is a highly acid substance (even the buffered form) and is irritating to the lining of the stomach. It must, therefore, always be preceded by food and milk.

2. Be on the alert for a side effect of ringing in the ears. This would indicate that you have exceeded the

maximum tolerable dose for your system.

3. Don't take aspirin if you have a history of stomach or duodenal ulcers.

Finally, a brief philosophical note. Let us not moan and groan too much about pain that occurs as a direct result of having fun, in sound mind and body. Let us not lose sight of the fact that literally millions of people spend their days in pain from things not even remotely related to enjoyment. It makes the aches a little bit easier to endure if we stop to remind ourselves of the difference.

PRACTICE GAMES

If you expect to achieve any significant improvement in racquetball, practice matches must be used for just that: **practice.** If you rely exclusively on your bread-and-butter shots during your practice games, you will never get any better. You will have to discipline yourself to work on some of your weaknesses, as well as new shots, every time you play. As a result, you will find yourself losing to a worthless hacker once in a while, and you will have to swallow some pride as he goes running out of the court broadcasting his hollow triumph to the whole club. The knowledge that you could have beaten him, if you had to, should sustain you at times like that. Keep your long-term objectives uppermost at all times. You will never develop a reliable backhand kill shot unless you are willing to hit a few thousand into the floor first. You can't possibly develop a well-rounded serving game, unless you are willing to learn by serving up a few pumpkins as you add new serves to your game. It is well worth it. What a great feeling of satisfaction you will have when you have successfully added a new dimension to your game. And when you beat the club champion, those meaningless past defeats will seem quite trivial in retrospect.

It's a terrible waste to go out on the court at any time without some definitive objectives in mind, other than winning, regardless of the relative strength of the other player. It is equally foolish to clutter your mind with too many things at the same time. You might think yourself right into oblivion, as is so well expressed in the Zen verse:

The centipede was happy, quite
Until a toad in fun
Said, "Pray, which leg goes after
  which?"
This worked his mind to such a pitch
He lay distracted in a ditch,
Considering how to run.

So why not select just two or three things to work on each time you play. The first time you might concentrate on hitting perfect left corner ceiling shots against all serves, and cross court kill shots on offense. The next time you might work on backhand kill shot serve returns and a variety of passing shots on offense. I would also recommend utilizing every match for the improvement of one or two serves. Always use a wide variety. But in order to upgrade the quality of each, select just one or two as your primary objectives every time you play. And don't be afraid to serve up a few right side serves to the local forehand kill shot artist. First of all, if the serve is well executed he will have a difficult shot to hit. Secondly, he is probably so unaccustomed to being served on the right that he will probably blow a few, which will surprise both you and him.

Now that the value of pre-match planning has been established, it takes very little argument to promote the equal value of post-game analysis. Playing without objectives is a waste. It is, perhaps, an even greater waste to play a practice match, hit 500-1000 shots, and then leave the court and forget about it. You must sit down some time later, and play the game over in your mind to some extent. Analyze your strengths and weaknesses, so that you can arrive at some plan for the next time out. Think about the quality of your play in every aspect of the game. Make yourself a check list of items to review after each match, something like this:

1. How many different serves were used? Which serves were placed well, and which need more work next time? Which serves led to kill shot returns?

2. How many points did you lose as a result of poor serve returns? How well were you able to move the server into the left corner with an accurate ceiling shot? Did you capitalize on (or even notice) his first move after he served?

3. How many of your passing shots reached the back wall before the second bounce? Did you always make a move after hitting a cross-court pass?

4. Did you shoot the backhand kill every time the chance was ripe? How many cross-court kill shots did you mix in? How many eventual winners did you get as a reward for perfect ceiling shots to the left corner?

I would venture to say that more than half of the players you meet don't have the faintest idea why they lose most of the time. If you can't figure out why you lose today, you're going to lose tomorrow. And tomorrow. And tomorrow.

Finally, a few unrelated suggestions regarding practice matches:

1. Try to play through without taking any timeouts, so as to build up your endurance as much as possible.

2. Don't play with weaker players before a tournament. Getting points you don't deserve tends to lead to sloppy play and poor shot selection. It's also no help to your conditioning.

3. Avoid playing with left-handers before a tournament, unless you expect to meet one. You would be practicing all the wrong shots with the usual backhand attack.

4. Play with a variety of players, so that your game will be challenged in as many different ways as possible.

PRACTICING ALONE

No matter how often you play racquetball competitively, you will not realize your full improvement potential until you occasionally spend some time practicing alone on the court. The very best time to practice a shot is immediately after you've missed it. You just don't have that chance during a match. It isn't necessary to practice very long under these conditions. If you can just spend thirty minutes by yourself hitting shots, you will have a productive session. But I do think it is necessary to have some outline or agenda in mind, in order to make the best use of your time. Try this for a start:

1. **Serves** — 5 minutes

    Hit a wide variety of serves, trying to perfect the subtle variations in height, speed and angle that make it impossible for the receiver to get "grooved". Hit a few short corner aces. This is a good serve to pull out of your bag when serving game or match point.

2. **Ceiling Shots** — 5 minutes

    Hit a wide variety of ceiling shots, but emphasize the backhand ceiling shot to the left corner, since that's the one you will be called upon to hit most often. Try to "wallpaper" it every time you hit one.

3. **Passing Shots** — 5 minutes

    Hit a mixture of the four basic passing shots, backhands and forehands, each to both sides. Pay close attention to the ultimate depth of the shots, noting whether or not they reach the backwall before the second bounce.

4. **Forehand Kill Shots** — 5 minutes

    Hit a variety of forehand kill shots from the five basic positional opportunities (see page 34) and don't forget to mix in a few to the left corner.

5. **Backhand Kill Shots** — 5 minutes

    Same exercise as in #4.

6. **Miscellaneous** — 5 minutes

    Spend the rest of the time working on the lesser shots, such as the Z-ball, drop shot, overhead kill, etc.

Finally, practice must be devoted to the goal of improvement. Don't make the typical golfer's error of spending your time "practicing" the very thing you are good at. Practice your **weakness,** not your strength. It's a lot more fun, as well as ego-building, to practice your strong points, but you won't get better that way. Most weekend golfers spend their practice time standing on the tee hitting 250 yard drives, which is a whale of a good time. Unfortunately, it isn't very productive or at all rewarding, because that wasn't their problem in the first place. They are probably losing 90% of their strokes on the close game. If they would just put away the big stick and spend an equal amount of time on chipping and putting, their scores would come down by five strokes. Take a lesson from the golf dummies. Apply a better line of thinking when you work on your racquetball skills. Work on your weakness.

If you can stand there and hit forehand rollouts with consistency, you should be practicing something else.

SCOUTING TO WIN

You will not always have the opportunity to watch an opponent in advance of a match. But if the opportunity is there, and you don't take it, you are missing a golden chance for some free information that you may have to pay dearly for later. And don't lose sight of your purpose. Don't just sit back and enjoy the game as if you were watching a parade. When you scout another player, you should have a definite list of questions on your mind, so that you can sit down afterwards, and privately jot down some concrete answers. Remember to resist your natural instincts, and watch the player instead of the ball.

Which serves does he usually hit? If he has a consistently good lob serve, you might plan to shake him up early by charging the serve and hitting it on the fly.

Does he have any unusual serves, such as the "wallpaper" serve, or the high-bounce Z-serve to the left corner? If so, you can prepare for these with five minutes of help from a friend.

What is his first move after each of his various serves? This is a very important point to observe, something that may be difficult to spot when you are in battle, watching the ball, getting ready to hit a return. You will be amazed to find some very good players with very bad positional habits, making them highly vulnerable to carefully selected serve returns. For example, most players have a good understanding of where to go after serving to the left corner, but have not yet convinced themselves that a right corner serve calls for the exact mirror image. They tend to drift to the left of center after serving to the right corner. This is poor position, and should be

punished with a down-the-wall pass.

The most common error you will observe is the server fading back too far after serving to either side, leaving himself vulnerable to a kill shot serve return. Make a note of it.

What serve returns will he usually hit against various serves? Some players always hit a kill shot if the serve comes off the back wall. These players can be set up like pigeons at a crucial time by simply serving a bit too deep, and moving forward toward the corner to re-kill the obvious return.

Where does he stand to receive serve? If it's only a step from the back wall, he is somewhat vulnerable to the short corner serve attempt, which might net you an easy ace on occasion.

You may also observe a specific weakness against one serve, such as a right corner Z-serve. These are all points worth noting on serve returns.

Which shots does he usually choose for winners? Most players will exhibit a definite pattern of shot selection, characteristic for certain situations. For example, on a set-up in the right front court on a ball coming off the back wall, most players will correctly choose the forehand kill shot to the right corner most of the time. These same players, faced with the identical chance on the left side, will cop out on the backhand kill shot, and go for the cross-court pass, instead. Watch for this. It may enable you to get a one-step advantage in either situation to save a point.

Does he mix in a few cross-court kill shots? If not, your worries are fewer.

Does he tend to shy away from hitting kill shots after he has missed a couple? If so, you can be ready to back off one whole step, at the appropriate time, to be in a better position for the pass.

Does he hit drop shots on close-in opportunities? What body language does he use to tip you off in advance?

What's his ceiling game like?

Does he become impatient after two or three exchanges, and try to get aggressive on the wrong shots?

Does he always go to the kill shot on a deep ceiling shot off the back wall? If so, you can be moving forward when you realize that your ceiling shot may be carrying too deep.

Does he hit any overhead kill shots or passes? Does he follow these shots forward?

Does he handle the right corner ceiling shot well, or does he have trouble angling it back to the left corner?

Does he begin to hang back in the backcourt after a few ceiling shot exchanges? If so, he is vulnerable to an occasional surprise overhead kill shot.

Does he provide any clues with his feet position or racquet position before he hits a kill shot? Does he bend the knees more on a backhand kill shot? Does he take a longer backstroke on a forehand kill shot? Does he cock the wrist more on a backhand kill?

After all of this meticulous dissection, you should be able to come away with a much better idea of how to nullify his strengths and illustrate his weaknesses. At the very least, you will spare yourself a few unnerving surprises.

Scouting should not, by all means, be reserved for the player who may be your upcoming opponent. It can be highly informative in three other respects:

1. Don't neglect the opportunity to scout a player that you play with regularly. You will see some things from off the court that you might never have noticed while playing, It will help you develop a more critical, watchful eye to analyze his game from the point of view of a stranger.

2. Watch the top players in action every chance you get, even if they represent a bracket you'll never get into. You might learn a few strategic maneuvers that you wouldn't see otherwise.

3. It can even be useful to do some scouting from a totally negative point of view. Watch a few lesser players. Take the point of view of a coach or critic. Ask yourself how you would beat him most easily, and what advice you would give him to improve. Thinking about coaching another player can teach you a lot about your own game.

In conclusion, scouting another player is potentially valuable, but only if approached in a thorough, methodical and analytical spirit. Most of your opponent's quirks and foibles will be apparent eventually as you play the match. And you will be using a similar analytical approach in feeling out an opponent early in the match. But why not observe some of these things in advance, before the score is 10-zip?

POSITIONAL DISCIPLINE

There is an optimum position on the court for every possible situation. This is the spot that uniquely combines the very best chance to retrieve any shot he might hit, with the very best chance to capitalize aggressively on a poor return.

Throughout this book, I have discussed what I feel to be the optimum position to be taken for various situations, such as receiving serve (see page 24), after serving to the left (see page 17), after hitting a ceiling shot (see page 20), after hitting a cross-court pass (see page 36), when your opponent is in trouble in the back court (see page 47), when he has a set-up forehand kill (see page 44), etc. Study the diagram and you'll see how often it is necessary to depart from a blind "center court" concept. (Diag. 25)

Some of the time you may be fortunate to know immediately after you hit the ball that you have hit a winner. You can just stand there and graciously bow to the cheers from the crowd. Most of the time, however, there remains at least a possibility that the shot will be retrieved. Related to this question, a negative state of mind brings positive results. Every time you hit a winner, no matter how well executed, assume that he will make a great get, and move. If you don't, you'll be left standing there waiting for the instant replay.

It requires a high degree of discipline and dedication to integrate into your game the unwavering habit of **always** heading for the optimum position after every shot you hit, no matter how good. The next time you receive those cheers, stop for a split second and ask yourself if you are standing on the spot that would have been the best position if he had gotten your shot back. If you are

not, you won't be hearing those cheers very often.

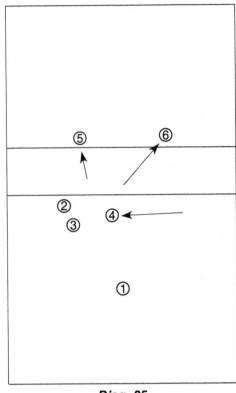

Diag. 25
1. To receive serve
2. After serving to left corner
3. After ceiling shot to left corner
4. After cross-court pass to the left
5. Opponent in trouble in left corner
6. Opponent has a forehand set-up

THE TWENTY COMMANDMENTS

1. Thou shalt not serve pumpkins.

2. Thou shalt not fade or drift after serving.

3. Thou shalt not stay in the center after serving to the corner.

4. Thou shalt not play back too far to receive serve.

5. Thou shalt not fail to recognize the most important shot in the game.

6. Thou shalt not fall asleep during a ceiling shot exchange.

7. Thou shalt not fail to use the ceiling shot to its utmost benefit.

8. Thou shalt not pass up a single chance to hit a winner.

9. Thou shalt not hit passing shots too high.

10. Thou shalt not wait for a bounce on all shots.

11. Thou shalt not hit a drop shot from above the knee.

12. Thou shalt not give up on the point after a bad shot.

13. Thou shalt not hit into the back wall unless there is no alternative.

14. Thou shalt hit no shot without a following move.

15. Thou shalt not be blind to body language.

16. Thou shalt not play without pre-game plans and post-game analyses.

17. Thou shalt not fail to alter your game to fit the opposition.

18. Thou shalt not practice without objectives.

19. Thou shalt never, never, never take your eye off the ball.

20. **Thou shalt think.**

AN ESSAY

I love racquetball.

I love racquetball because I have a desire to win.

I love racquetball because I am not a great athlete.

I love racquetball because it is a sport which gives me a chance to beat a better athlete.

I love racquetball because I have no chance to beat a golfer who can hit the ball farther and putt better than I, but I do have a chance to beat a racquetball player who can hit better kill shots and passing shots than I, if he hits them at the wrong time.

I love racquetball because I can beat a player who can hit kill shots with 100% accuracy, by preventing him from hitting kill shots. 100% of nothin' is nothin'.

I love racquetball because you have to think to win.

I love racquetball.

PLAY REGULATIONS

RULE I—Serve-Generally.

(a) Order. The player or side winning the toss becomes the first server and starts the first game, and the third game, if any.

(b) Start. Games are started from any place in the service zone. No part of either foot may extend beyond either line of the service zone. Stepping on the line (but not beyond it) is permitted. Server must remain in the service zone until the served ball passes short line. Violations are called "foot faults."

(c) Manner. A serve is commenced by bouncing the ball to the floor in the service zone, and on the first bounce the ball is struck by the server's racquet so that it hits the front wall and on the rebound hits the floor back of the short line, either with or without touching one of the side walls.

(d) Readiness. Serves shall not be made until the receiving side is ready, or the referee has called play ball.

RULE II—Serve-In Doubles.

(a) Server. At the beginning of each game in doubles, each side shall inform the referee of the order of service, which order shall be followed throughout the game. Only the first server serves the first time up and continues to serve first throughout the game. When the first server is out—the side is out. Thereafter both players on each side shall serve until a hand-out occurs. It is not necessary for the server to alternate serves to their opponents.

(b) Partner's Position. On each serve, the server's partner shall stand erect with his back to the side wall and with both feet on the floor within the service box until the served ball passes the short line. Violations are called "foot faults."

RULE III—Defective Serves.

Defective serves are of three types resulting in penalties as follows:

(a) Dead Ball Serve. A dead ball serve results in no penalty and the server is given another serve without cancelling a prior illegal serve.

(b) Fault Serve. Two fault serves results in a hand-out.

(c) Out Serves. An out serve results in a hand-out.

RULE IV—Dead Ball Serves.

Dead ball serves do not cancel any previous illegal serve. They occur when an otherwise legal serve:

(a) Hits Partner. Hits the server's partner on the fly on the rebound from the front wall while the server's partner is in the service box. Any serve that touches the floor before hitting the partner in the box is a short.

(b) Screen Balls. Passes too close to the server or the server's partner to obstruct the view of the returning side. Any serve passing behind the server's partner and the side wall is an automatic screen.

(c) Court Hinders. Hits any part of the court that under local rules is a dead ball.

RULE V—Fault Serves.

The following serves are faults and any two in succession results in a hand-out:

(a) Foot Faults. A foot fault results:

(1) When the server leaves the service zone before the served ball passes the short line.

(2) When the server's partner leaves the service box before the served ball passes the short line.

(b) Short Serve. A short serve is any served ball that first hits the front wall and on the rebound hits the floor in front of the back edge of the short line either with or without touching one side wall.

(c) Two-Side Serve. A two-side serve is any ball served that first hits the front wall and on the rebound hits two side walls on the fly.

(d) Ceiling Serve. A ceiling serve is any served ball that touches the ceiling after hitting the front wall either with or without touching one side wall.

(e) Long Serve. A long serve is any served ball that first hits the front wall and rebounds to the back wall before touching the floor.

(f) Out of Court Serve. Any ball going out of the court on the serve.

RULE VI—Out Serves.

Any one of the following serves results in a hand-out:

(a) Bounces. Bouncing the ball more than three times while in the service zone before striking the ball. A bounce is a drop or throw to the floor, followed by a catch. The ball may not be bounced anywhere but on the floor within the serve zone. Accidental dropping of the ball counts as one bounce.

(b) Missed Ball. Any attempt to strike the ball on the first bounce that results either in a total miss or in touching any part of the server's body other than his racquet.

(c) Non-front Serve. Any served ball that strikes the server's partner, or the ceiling, floor or side wall, before striking the front wall.

(d) Touched Serve. Any served ball that on the rebound from the front wall touches the server, or touches the server's partner while any part of his body is out of the service box, or the server's partner intentionally catches the served ball on the fly.

(e) Out-of-Order Serve. In doubles, when either partner serves out of order.

(f) Crotch Serve. If the served ball hits the crotch in the front wall it is considered the same as hitting the floor and is an out. A crotch serve into the back wall is good and in play.

RULE VII—Return of the Serve.

(a) Receiving Position. The receiver or receivers must stand at least 5 feet back of the short line, as indicated by the 3 inch vertical line on each side wall, and cannot return the ball until it passes the short line. Any infraction results in a point for the server.

(b) Defective Serve. To eliminate any misunderstanding, the receiving side should not catch or touch a defectively served ball until called by the referee or it has touched the floor the second time.

(c) Fly Return. In making a fly return the receiver must end up with both feet back of the service zone. A violation by a receiver results in a point for the server.

(d) Legal Return. After the ball is legally served, one of the players on the receiving side must strike the ball with his racquet either on the fly or after the first bounce and before the ball touches the floor the second time to return the ball to the front wall either directly or after touching one or both side walls, the back wall or the ceiling, or any combination of those surfaces. A returned ball may not touch the floor before touching the front wall. It is legal to return the ball by striking it into the back wall first, then hitting the front wall on the fly or after hitting the side wall or ceiling.

(e) Failure to Return. The failure to return a serve results in a point for the server.

RULE VIII—Changes of Serve.

(a) Hand-out. A server is entitled to continue serving until:

(1) Out Serve. He makes an out serve under Rule VI, or

(2) Fault Serves. He makes two fault serves in succession under Rule V, or

(3) Hits Partner. He hits his partner with an attempted return before the ball touches the floor the second time, or

(4) Return Failure. He or his partner fails to keep the ball in play by returning it as required by Rule VII (d), or

(5) Avoidable Hinder. He or his partner commits an avoidable hinder under Rule XI.

(b) Side-out.

(1) In Singles. In singles, retiring the server retires the side.

(2) In Doubles. In doubles, the side is retired when both partners have been put out, except on the first serve as provided in Rule II (a).

(c) Effect. When the server on the side loses the serve, the server or serving side shall become the receiver; and the receiving side, the server; and so alternately in all subsequent services of the game.

RULE IX—Volleys.

Each legal return after the serve is called a volley. Play during volleys shall be according to the following rules:

(a) One or Both Hands. Only the head of the racquet may be used at any time to return the ball. The ball must be hit with the racquet in one or both hands. Switching hands to hit a ball is an out. The use of any portion of the body is an out.

(b) One Touch. In attempting returns, the ball may be touched only once by one player on returning side. In doubles both partners may swing at, but only one, may hit the ball. Each violation of (a) or (b) results in a hand-out or point.

(c) Return Attempts.

(1) In Singles. In singles if a player swings at but misses the ball in play, the player may repeat his attempts to return the ball until it touches the floor the second time.

(2) In Doubles. In doubles if one player swings at but misses the ball, both he and his partner may make further attempts to return the ball until it touches the floor the second time. Both partners on a side are entitled to an attempt to return the ball.

(3) Hinders. In singles or doubles, if a player swings at but misses the ball in play, and in his, or his partner's attempt again to play the ball there is an unintentional interference by an opponent it shall be a hinder. (See Rule X.)

(d) Touching the Ball. Except as provided in Rule X (a)(2), any touching of a ball before it touches the floor the second time by a player other than the one making a return is a point or out against the offending player.

(e) Out-of-Court Ball.

(1) After Return. Any ball returned to the front wall which on the rebound or on the first bounce goes into the gallery or through any opening in a side wall shall be declared dead and the serve replayed.

(2) No Return. Any ball not returned to the front wall, but which caroms off a player's racquet into the gallery or into any opening in a side wall either with or without

touching the ceiling, side or back wall, shall be an out or point against the players failing to make the return.

(f) Dry Ball. During the game and particularly on service every effort should be made to keep the ball dry. Deliberately wetting shall result in an out. The ball may be inspected by the referee at any time during a game.

(g) Broken Ball. If there is any suspicion that a ball has broken on the serve or during a volley, play shall continue until the end of the volley. The referee or any player may request the ball be examined. If the referee decides the ball is broken or otherwise defective, a new ball shall be put into play and the point replayed.

(h) Play Stoppage. Play stops:

(1) If a player loses a shoe or other equipment, or foreign objects enter the court, or any other outside interference occurs, the referee shall stop the play.

(2) If a player loses control of his racquet, time should be called after the point has been decided, providing the racquet does not strike an opponent or interfere with ensuing play.

RULE X—Dead Ball Hinders.

Hinders are of two types—"dead ball" and "avoidable." Dead ball hinders as described in this rule result in the point being replayed. Avoidable hinders are described in Rule XI.

(a) Situations. When called by the referee, the following are dead ball hinders:

(1) Court Hinders. Hits any part of the court which under local rules is a dead ball.

(2) Hitting Opponent. Any returned ball that touches an opponent on the fly before it returns to the front wall.

(3) Body Contact. Any body contact with an opponent that interferes with seeing or returning the ball.

(4) Screen Ball. Any ball rebounding from the front wall close to the body of a player on the side which just returned the ball, to interfere with or prevent the

returning side from seeing the ball. See Rule IV (b).

(5) Straddle Ball. A ball passing between the legs of a player on the side which just returned the ball, if there is no fair chance to see or return the ball.

(6) Other Interference. Any other unintentional interference which prevents an opponent from having a fair chance to see or return the ball.

(b) Effect. A call by the referee of a "hinder" stops the play and voids any situation following, such as the ball hitting a player. No player is authorized to call a hinder, except on the back swing and such a call must be made immediately.

(c) Avoidance. While making an attempt to return the ball, a player is entitled to a fair chance to see and return the ball. It is the duty of the side that has just served or returned the ball to move so that the receiving side may go straight to the ball and not be required to go around an opponent. The referee should be liberal in calling hinders to discourage any practice of playing the ball where an adversary cannot see it until too late. It is no excuse that the ball is "killed," unless in the opinion of the referee he couldn't return the ball. Hinders should be called without a claim by a player, especially in close plays and on game points.

(d) In Doubles. In doubles, both players on a side are entitled to a fair and unobstructed chance at the ball and either one is entitled to a hinder even though it naturally would be his partner's ball and even though his partner may have attempted to play the ball or that he may already have missed it. It is not a hinder when one player hinders his partner.

RULE XI—Avoidable Hinders.

An avoidable hinder results in an "out" or a point depending upon whether the offender was serving or receiving.

(a) Failure to Move. Does not move sufficiently to allow opponent his shot.

(b) Blocking. Moves into a position effecting a block, on the opponent about to return the ball, or, in doubles, one partner moves in front of an opponent as his partner is returning the ball.

(c) Moving Into Ball. Moves in the way and is struck by the ball just played by his opponent.

(d) Pushing. Deliberately pushing or shoving an opponent during a volley.

RULE XII—Rest Periods.

(a) Delays. Deliberate delay exceeding ten seconds by server, or receiver, shall result in an out or point against the offender.

(b) During Game. During a game each player in singles, or each side in doubles, either while serving or receiving may request a "time out" for a towel, wiping glasses, change or adjustment. Each "time out" shall not exceed 30 seconds. No more than three "time outs" in a game shall be granted each singles player or each team in doubles.

(c) Injury. No time out shall be charged to a player who is injured during play. An injured player shall not be allowed more than a total of 15 minutes of rest. If the injured player is not able to resume play after total rests of 15 minutes the match shall be awarded to the opponent or opponents. On any further injury to same player, the Commissioner, if present, or committee, after considering any available medical opinion shall determine whether the injured player will be allowed to continue.

(d) Between Games. A 5 minute rest period is allowed between the first and second games and a 10 minute rest period between the second and third games. Players may leave the court between games, but must be on the court and ready to play at the expiration of the rest period.

(e) Postponed Games. Any games postponed by referee due to weather elements shall be resumed with the same score as when postponed.

Play Regulations section reprinted courtesy of the United States Racquetball Association.